BY DUTY BOUND

MICHELLE RAY

Quills & Quartos
PUBLISHING

Copyright © 2024 by Michelle Ray

All rights reserved.

This is a work of fiction. Names, characters, businesses, places, events, locales, and incidents are either the products of the author's imagination or used in a fictitious manner. Any resemblance to actual persons, living or dead, or actual events is purely coincidental.

No part of this book may be reproduced in any form or by any electronic or mechanical means, including information storage and retrieval systems, without written permission from the author, except for the use of brief quotations in a book review.

No AI training. Without in any way limiting the author's [and publisher's] exclusive rights under copyright, any use of this publication to "train" generative artificial intelligence (AI) technologies to generate text is expressly prohibited. The author reserves all rights to license uses of this work for generative AI training and development of machine learning language models.

Ebooks are for the personal use of the purchaser. You may not share or distribute this ebook in any way, to any other person. To do so is infringing on the copyright of the author, which is against the law.

Edited by Jan Ashton and Regina McCaughey-Silvia

Cover by Beetiful Book Covers

ISBN 978-1-956613-96-4 (ebook) and 978-1-956613-97-1 (paperback)

To Wendy, who will be missed and loved forever

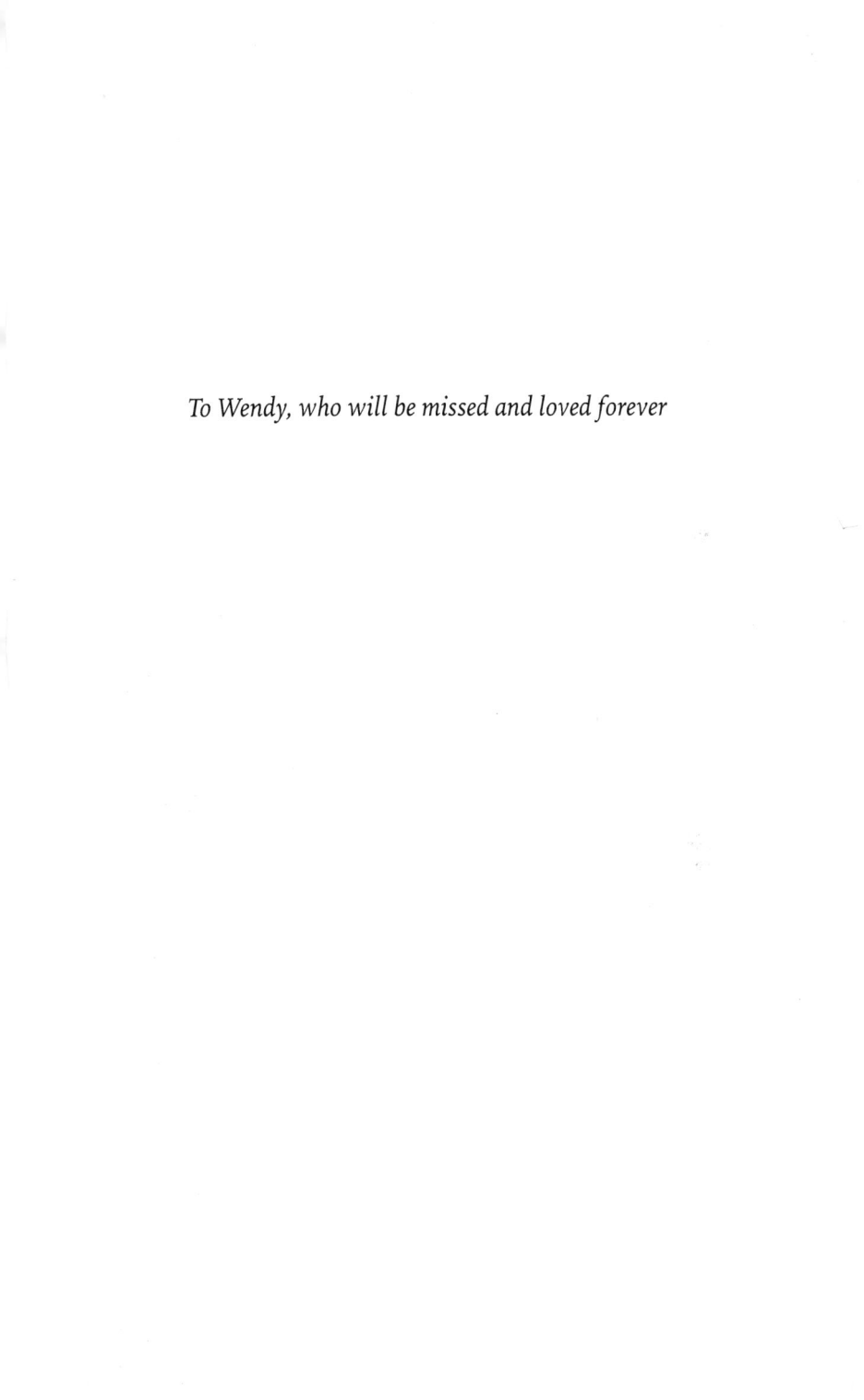

CONTENTS

Chapter 1	1
Chapter 2	6
Chapter 3	11
Chapter 4	19
Chapter 5	25
Chapter 6	36
Chapter 7	45
Chapter 8	54
Chapter 9	62
Chapter 10	72
Chapter 11	77
Chapter 12	84
Chapter 13	91
Chapter 14	101
Chapter 15	106
Chapter 16	118
Chapter 17	126
Chapter 18	135
Chapter 19	142
Chapter 20	150
Chapter 21	162
Chapter 22	168
Chapter 23	176
Chapter 24	185
Chapter 25	191
Chapter 26	203
Chapter 27	212
Chapter 28	220
Chapter 29	228
Chapter 30	237

Chapter 31	248
Chapter 32	253
Epilogue	263
Acknowledgments	273
About the Author	275
Also by Michelle Ray	277

CHAPTER 1

Summer 1809

We arrived late to the assembly because my favourite blue dress had gone missing. It was eventually located in Kitty's wardrobe. Kitty swore she had not borrowed it, and while at first I was inclined to believe she had, in fact, turned thief (for coveting Jane's and my possessions had led to her occasionally hiding them away), she reminded us that, unlike my ball gown or my pearl hair pin, this dress was not one she admired. She went so far as to say she found it unbecoming and doubted I would secure a husband if I continued to wear it.

As much as we hurried, by the time we arrived at the assembly, the hall was crowded and overheated. Despite Jane's suggestion that we return home—arguing that there would be no one new to meet and we might swoon before we found refreshments or an agreeable partner—we entered. I pretended as best I could to conceal my headache, knowing Jane would use it as another reason to suggest we depart, but the temperature and lack of air would make for an excruciating evening.

We pushed our way through the crowd and spotted Charlotte Lucas beckoning us. As soon as we were near, she said, "A traveller has come to the assembly!"

"You see?" I said, elbowing Jane's ribs. "There is someone new to meet, though for all we know he may be appalling in both manners and appearance." Jane laughed.

Charlotte pointed in the direction of a small group in the corner, but I could see no faces. The music had paused, and laughter was loud throughout the room.

Then the man turned around. He was slim and of medium height, had thick, light brown hair, a smooth face with a pointed chin, and a bearing that gave him out to be of noble blood. He was speaking with our neighbours, the Gouldings and the Lucases. The man, soon followed by Sir William and Mr Goulding, began walking in our direction.

"Heavens," Charlotte said under her breath, and I was unsure whether she welcomed or dreaded the impending introduction.

"Charlotte, fear not," I said. "He is just a man." Ever since we were young, she had blushed and stammered at the very thought of any man speaking with her, and belittled herself when I brought up the many virtues that made her an attractive potential wife.

Charlotte's colour rose as her father neared, and she hid her face with a premature curtsey.

Sir William cleared his throat, but Charlotte kept her face lowered even after she had risen from the too-deep curtsey. His eyes darted to mine, and I offered the most imperceptible shrug I could manage. He said, "Mr Fitzwilliam, my daughter, Miss Lucas."

At this point she darted a glance upwards, her face even redder than before, and Mr Fitzwilliam bowed in return.

Next, Mr Goulding introduced Jane and then me, explaining that his son's friend from Cambridge, Mr Darcy, had brought Mr Fitzwilliam to their estate, Haye-Park and had intended to come to the assembly with him, but remained back as he was feeling unwell.

Sir William asked, "And where is your son?"

Mr Goulding looked over his shoulder, "He went for refreshments some time ago." He shrugged. "Young men are distracted by curricles and beautiful faces, are they not?"

The men laughed as I looked about to see if the young man in question had indeed found a beautiful face to be distracted by. Mr William Goulding was handsome, but had never held any attraction for me or for Jane. His spirit was too wild. Perhaps being a cosseted son in a large family had allowed for such spirit, much as my younger sisters had been allowed to play and shout at will. Regardless, he was kind and amusing, but not a man to whom I desired any permanent attachment.

Mr Fitzwilliam attempted to pay equal attention to each lady as Mr Goulding and Sir William spoke briefly of his and our family lineages and long friendship, as well as Meryton's better qualities, but Mr Fitzwilliam's eyes returned to Jane over and over as if pulled by a power beyond his control. Jane, however, said nothing.

"What brings you to Meryton?" I asked him.

"I..." He seemed unable to form words, and I began to wonder whether he had all his wits. But when Jane dropped her gaze to the floor, it released him from her spell, and he turned to me, straightening his shoulders, and beaming proudly. "I have been travelling with my cousin Darcy for a bit of adventure before I join the Regulars. Seeing Goulding at Haye-Park is our last stop before London. Had you met me a month hence, I should have been introduced as Colonel Fitzwilliam."

Jane lifted her gaze and said, "How marvellous," and he was lost to her once again.

Sir William said something that the future colonel seemed not to hear. He repeated himself, and Mr Fitzwilliam said, "Yes, of course. The next dance does belong to Miss Lucas." And though he put out an elbow to escort Charlotte, he could not help but glance once more at Jane.

Our mother approached, asking Sir William whether Mr Fitzwilliam had been properly introduced to us, then proceeded to ask him about the stranger, giving Jane the opportunity to quietly confide in me that she found Mr Fitzwilliam excessively handsome.

Having overheard, Mama interrupted. "Indeed, he is. And if he can buy his way into the Regulars as a colonel, his family must have money."

"Mama!" Jane looked about to see who might have heard this outrageous comment.

Thus it was, and it seemed thus would ever be. My mother's incessant queries, delivered in a voice that all could hear, always humiliated us, and could easily drive away our prospects.

"Lizzy," Mama asked, interrupting my glum musings. "Are you quite well?"

I had clapped my eyes shut and was pressing fingertips against my temples, and though I did not wish to admit it, said, "My head is feeling very ill."

"We should return home," Jane said immediately.

My mother scowled at me as if I had concocted this pain to ruin her evening. "You cannot leave!"

"We cannot stay," Jane replied immediately. "Not with Lizzy feeling ill."

"We must," I argued, knowing Jane could not depart before she and Mr Fitzwilliam had had their dance—entertainment and new suitors were in short supply in Meryton. She appeared as if she would like to argue more but I forestalled her, saying, "Perhaps only *I* could return home. Mr Fitzwilliam seems rather impressed with you, Jane. You ought to remain."

Mama tsked. "Well of course he is! A man could go a long way and never see beauty like Jane's."

Sir William's lips pressed into a line as he looked over his shoulder at his daughter, dancing happily with Mr Fitzwilliam, though it was impossible not to notice the gentleman's constant glances in our direction.

After a few perfunctory farewells, I was at last in the carriage, my head resting upon the cool glass of the window for the short journey back to Longbourn.

CHAPTER 2

"Lizzy. Lizzy!" My mother's voice pierced the air, an unmerciful jolt out of slumber.

"Mama, leave me be," I moaned, reluctantly opening my eyes. I had slept late to chase away the pain, even past Jane's return to our room after the assembly's end.

"Oh, your head! Did we not hear enough about your head last night?" My mother threw open the curtains and I noted the dark grey of the clouds and streaks of rain upon the windows. "What do I care about your head when a man of importance has come to visit!"

I sat up on my elbows, noting the pain was more of a dull ache than the throbbing it had been the night prior. "What man?"

"Mr Fitzwilliam, of course!" She fluttered to my wardrobe. "Bridget will be up to dress you. He is in with your father, giving Jane a moment to gather herself."

"He is here for *Jane*. Can I not remain in bed?"

She scowled and said, "Ridiculous!" Then she fluttered

out to the hall. At moments such as these, I could imagine what she was like as a girl.

Sitting up fully, I stretched, noting the rain clacking against the windowpanes, and considered what to wear.

I was sorry I had not been awake when Jane had returned to our bedchamber last night, for I should have much preferred knowing what she thought of Mr Fitzwilliam before our father met him and our mother grew excited over his call at Longbourn. When I entered the drawing room, Jane and Mr Fitzwilliam were sipping tea, darting bashful glances at each other as our father asked about his father's library.

"I—" He sneezed with such force that the teacup clattered, sloshing liquid into the saucer. He stood to mark my entrance, and another sneeze came as he bowed. I noticed he was soaked, and a blanket had been placed under him on the sofa to preserve it.

I curtseyed and gestured to him to take his seat again. "Mr Fitzwilliam, did you walk here?"

"I thought it might be restorative after last night's festivities, but I only seem"—he paused as another sneeze came forth—"to have exposed myself to the rain and caught a cold." He set his saucer down and pulled a handkerchief from his pocket, attempting to blow delicately. The smile he offered was wan, and his cheeks were flushed. "The walk from Haye-Park was longer than I anticipated, given the weather."

"Mr Fitzwilliam," said my mother, "did you find the assembly pleasing?"

"Yes. The company especially." His eyes flicked to Jane, who blushed and looked at her lap. "In town, the gatherings are typically too formal for my taste, and at Rosings Park—my aunt's estate in Kent—I find I know the guests too well to enjoy but a few."

My father chuckled at that.

Mr Fitzwilliam pressed the back of his hand to his forehead. "I am afraid I have developed a fever. I ought to—" He began to rise but fell back upon the sofa. "Pardon me. I am unwell."

I looked to my parents, but they made no offer of comfort or a solution. I said, "Perhaps he could borrow some dry things of Papa's and rest for a while in a guest room?"

"Of course!" My mother leapt to her feet, spurred to demonstrate our household's expert hospitality. "Jane, tell Mrs Hill to ready hot water. Mr Bennet, send John to find some appropriate attire for Mr Fitzwilliam. I shall tell Hill to prepare a room." All of these tasks might have been simply directed through Hill to pass on as she saw fit, but my mother either enjoyed the excitement or else could not think clearly enough in a crisis to have realised. I suspected both might be true.

Moments later, Mr Fitzwilliam and I were left alone, and he sneezed again. Footsteps hurried overhead and hysterical voices echoed down the hall. I attempted not to grimace, but Mr Fitzwilliam had closed his eyes, lost to his discomfort, and seemed not to notice.

"Shall we send word to Haye-Park of your condition?" I enquired.

Unaccountably the question made him rise to his feet. "Haye-Park. Yes, that would be—" He staggered, grabbing onto the back of a chair.

"Mr Fitzwilliam! Hill! Papa! Come quick!" I hurried to Mr Fitzwilliam, taking him around the waist in an attempt to hold him up. My father hurried into the room and I cried, "Help me! He seems to have— Do gentlemen swoon?"

My father approached the near senseless man and took his arm, pulling it around his shoulder. "Let us get you upstairs."

Slurring his words as his head bobbed, Mr Fitzwilliam said, "I would not wish to be a bother."

"You are ill, sir. Not another word."

"A single man is staying in our home. How scandalous!" Kitty said, and she and Lydia burst into peals of giggles at the dinner table.

"Do not be absurd," I said, reaching for a glass.

My mother fanned herself. "Oh heavens, she has a point. What if this was published widely? Would our girls be ruined?"

"For allowing an ill guest to stay in our home?" asked my father. "Pray, do not be ridiculous. There is no harm in being hospitable. Would they have us turn him out into the road?"

"Ought we to notify his companion?" I asked. "Mr… Darcy, was it not?"

"Yes," said Papa. "I shall send word to him at the Goulding's at once."

The rest of the meal was spent in speculation, mostly indelicate, about Mr Fitzwilliam's life, as well as his interest in Jane. I hoped the words did not carry clearly up to the guest room. Papa retired to his study to craft a note to Mr Fitzwilliam's friend, saying he ought not to worry and to come on the morrow so as to avoid being soaked in the ongoing storm.

CHAPTER 3

An entire day of rain had me anxious for fresh air and movement, so the next morning, I ventured out at an early hour. The clouds hung so low that it seemed as if one could touch them. Drawn skyward, I climbed the hill that overlooked Meryton, hoping not to displease Hill by making a mess of my boots and hem, as I was wont to do.

The climb felt steeper, as the incline was slick upon my ascent. At the crest, I admired Longbourn and Netherfield to one side and Haye-Park to the other. Even far off, Haye-Park's brick turrets stood out upon the green expanse where sheep grazed.

I picked my way down the hill, stopping to speak with a tenant whose wife had just given birth to another healthy child. A boy, this time, which pleased the man. After bidding each other farewell, I continued down, gathering wildflowers from the side of the road for Mama. She loved cultivated roses from her garden best, but enjoyed being thought of with the untamed beauty of my bouquets. I was reaching for a particularly lovely blossom when I lost my footing and slipped backwards. My arms windmilled as I fell, and a strangled scream escaped my throat as I landed on the ground. I moved to stand only to find myself once again slipping, this time landing in a puddle deep enough to cover my boots to the ankle. Letting loose a growl of frustration at having lost my bouquet, I turned my head to see petals and stems littering the path of my descent. Then I began to laugh. What else could I do?

The back of my skirt and entire hem were caked in mud—a problem, unfortunately, which would become the task of our laundry maid. I made my way back up, hoping to rescue some of the flowers, enough to make a much smaller bouquet. I took up a few and threw others to the side, for they were crushed beyond usefulness. As I reached the last one, a figure appeared on the hill. He was tall, well-dressed, and had a regal bearing.

"Tread carefully, sir," I called.

The man slowed, yet with his long legs he quickly reached where I stood. "I am looking for Longbourn. Would that be the house there?"

"Indeed. Are you, perchance, Mr Darcy?"

He bowed his head in greeting. "I am."

I could not help but note the strength of his jaw and the handsome swoop of dark brown hair across his brow. "Your cousin, Mr Fitzwilliam, has been recovering with us."

"And you are?"

"Miss Elizabeth Bennet."

"The second daughter of the house, I believe."

I nodded, noticing as I did that he seemed to be

observing the condition of my skirts and petticoats. His eyes sparkled with mischief as he said, "It must have been quite a puddle of mud into which you fell."

I regarded my ruined dress and grinned. "It was indeed. The puddle was the end. It began with a slip and a slide. I assure you, it was most indelicate, and I am relieved I was alone whilst taking such a tumble." The smile he returned caused my stomach to flip, and it took a moment longer than I would have liked to say, "Please, sir, this way."

As we walked, Mr Darcy asked, "Is Fitzwilliam's condition grave? Mr Bennet's note said only that it was a fever, which could mean anything, and I feared, could have been false reassurance."

"Your cousin is rather ill. We thought it was just a chill, but this morning his fever had grown worse."

"Have you called a physician?"

"Mr Fitzwilliam insisted it was not necessary, but you might convince him to allow that at least our apothecary, Mr Jones, comes to see him."

Mr Darcy frowned but nodded. "My cousin can be stubborn."

We entered the house. Mr Darcy's eyes drifted about, taking stock of the ceilings and the chandeliers, to the doorway of the sitting room and, to my dismay, the crack in the wall of the entry—the one I had asked my father to have fixed no fewer than four times in the past month.

"Miss Elizabeth, what on earth happened to you?" Mrs Hill had hurried in to meet our guest.

"A fall. No cause for panic."

Her eyes settled on my filthy skirt and narrowed

further. Her mouth opened as if she might reprimand me, but settled for seeing to tea while I invited Mr Darcy into the sitting room.

"Would it be possible for me to be shown to Fitzwilliam immediately?"

"Yes, of course. I shall escort you to him." As we walked up the stairs, I could hear Kitty and Lydia arguing in their room. I hoped Mr Darcy did not notice, but when Lydia shrieked, he startled. I forced myself to laugh, though inside I was wretched, wondering what he thought of our family already. Immediately on the heels of that thought was wonder that I should care about the opinion of a man I had only just met. "My younger sisters are spirited and often bicker. Have you any brothers or sisters?"

Another shriek—this one from Kitty—was followed by a thud. I hoped it was a book or a chair and not one of the girls.

"I have an older brother, Thomas, and a younger sister, Georgiana."

"Do you fight?" I feared my query might be regarded as too personal, but he did not hesitate to answer.

"With my brother, yes. Thomas is tremendously competitive. Even now he always strives to win, though it no longer leads to physical altercations."

"And your sister?"

We were almost at the door, and I wished to speak more to him. I could not understand why, but I desired to know all there was to know about this man.

"Georgiana was still young when I went to university. She is twelve years my junior—still a girl, really." His face softened as he spoke of her. "Our relationship has always been affectionate rather than quarrelsome. I have missed her dearly on my travels."

"Your travels?"

"Fitzwilliam and I have been travelling in anticipation of his accepting his commission. A last burst of fire if you will."

To my disappointment, we had reached Mr Fitzwilliam's bedchamber. I gestured towards the door. "Your cousin is within."

A faint groan came from the other side of the door. I moved out of the way so Mr Darcy could enter and then excused myself.

"Thank you," he said. His eyes locked onto mine, and I noticed their dazzling beauty: a deep green with hints of blue, shining like jewels. "You have been very kind."

It was a moment before I was able to speak. "I shall await you in the drawing room."

An hour later, Mr Darcy entered the drawing room where I sat with my entire family. "How fares our guest?" my father enquired.

Mr Darcy smiled and nodded in reply to my mother's offer of tea. "He does very poorly, sir, but is quite certain he wants only for time to recover."

"Mr Fitzwilliam said you were travelling," my mother said as she poured. "Was it for business or for pleasure?"

"A bit of both. When I was young, I dreamt of going on a Grand Tour, but with the war raging, that was an impossibility. I went to Cambridge first, hoping the war would end soon. Alas, it has not, but my cousin and I still wished to have a bit of adventure before he accepts his commission, so we have been all about Wales, Scotland, Ireland, and England."

"Tell me how you found Scotland," my father said. "I have always dreamt of walking the Highlands."

"Oh, Mr Bennet," interrupted my mother, "can you imagine the two of us walking up and down hills together? I would tire easily and then where would we be?"

"I did not say we would go together," he muttered, and Mr Darcy stifled a laugh.

Mr Darcy shared tales of his travels, which proved too dull for Mama and the younger girls; they retreated to the sofa near the window to do needlework. I listened, appreciating his descriptions and details of various relics and areas of note, and the changing nature of the people from region to region, as well as their unique dress and customs.

"If I could," I said, "I would love to travel the globe. I long to see more than this little patch of the world."

Mary looked up from her Bible for the first time in nearly an hour. "'But godliness with contentment is great gain.'"

Mr Darcy cocked his head and looked at my sister. Many dismissed Mary outright for her pedantic nature and serious air, so I feared what he might say. "Is that not the same passage of Timothy that ends with, 'For the love of money is the root of all evil'?"

Lydia, who had been sashaying across the room to

make the ribbons on her dress float out, cried, "That is a kind of evil I strive for!"

"I do, as well," said Kitty with a laugh.

Mr Darcy looked to me, amusement dancing in his eyes, and I suspected he was recalling their shrieking upstairs as we had approached Mr Fitzwilliam's room. "I believe, Miss Mary," he said, his voice warm, "that travel can, in fact, make one appreciate what one has at home. Of course, seeing God's majesty in the rolling hills and thick woods and roaring rivers lifts the spirit and connects one to the Almighty."

Her cheeks pinkened and she went back to reading. A casual observer might have mistaken this for dismissiveness or disappointment, but as her sister, I suspected she, too, was captivated by his courtesy and good looks.

"If you had a choice, Miss Elizabeth, where would you like to travel?"

My mind whirled as I imagined the many places I had read of. "Italy. The Holy Land. India. France. Anywhere." I laughed. "I would settle for London."

"Have you not been to London before?"

"Once—no, twice. When I was younger. My aunt and uncle live there but generally come to see us in the country."

"I am surprised," he said mildly. "It is mere hours away."

My eyes flicked to Mama and Papa, whose looks were confusion and surprise, respectively. How to explain that my mother loathed travel, as it wore on her nerves, and my father preferred a quiet life with his books and that he often said town was full of nincompoops. "Yes, well, I hope to avail myself of my relations' hospitality in the future."

There was more to say about how protective my parents had been of me and of Jane, all while they fairly ignored—or in my mother's case *encouraged*—Kitty and Lydia's outlandish behaviour. They were excessively young, only thirteen and fifteen, but I would not be surprised if she packed them up and sent them to town even so.

Papa saved me from adding more detail by asking about Mr Darcy's family home.

"Pemberley? Yes, well..." Mr Darcy's face grew ashen. "It is well appointed but I prefer exploring."

How strange. He had been lively and relaxed, but once his family home was mentioned, he was altered completely.

He sipped his tea. "I had hoped to continue with our travels, but my catching cold, followed now by Fitzwilliam's illness, have quashed that. He must report for duty in a week. We were meant to stay with the Gouldings for only one night but I fear we may need to remain the entire week."

One week. Only one week before they had to depart. Or sooner, perhaps, if Mr Fitzwilliam recovered quickly. Why did this distress me so?

Mr Darcy asked Papa for a tour of his library, and my father was only too happy to oblige.

CHAPTER 4

The next morning, I walked out early into the woods just past the garden, not desiring anyone to see me. I wandered up and down various rises listening to the birds chirp, thankful for a warm morning as I had neglected to bring so much as a shawl. A thick tree had fallen some years back at the top of a rise, and it was my ongoing pleasure to climb upon it and leap off. Given my fall the day prior, however, I decided to remain on *terra firma*.

Movement to the side startled me. "Oh! Mr Darcy!"

His eyes were wide; evidently I had surprised him as well. "Excuse me. I-I was out for a walk and lost the path."

"In which direction were you going?" When he merely looked about, I asked, "Towards or away from Meryton?"

"Away. It is not much of a town, and its entertainments are not for me."

A laugh escaped my lips. So few people I met were as blunt as he, and it was both surprising and refreshing. "I quite agree." When he said nothing more, I added, "I was hoping for solitude today."

He reared back slightly. "Then I ought not to ask if I might join you." His sentence ended with a hint of disappointment.

"I..." I did not wish to be rude, though I had meant, as I said, to be alone. Yet, despite what others might say of me, I was not entirely without grace. "You may join me, as I meant I wished to be away from my sisters. At times their noise overwhelms me."

"I can imagine."

I looked sharply at him, and he cleared his throat and stepped closer to me. "My house, you see, was always a much quieter place. My older brother is a serious sort, and my younger sister was still in the nursery, as I explained, when I left for school. My parents were often abroad, and when home, they were, well, uninterested in games or conversation. So you see, I am not accustomed to much noise or intrusion."

"Was it lonely?"

He pressed his lips together and looked down.

Ah. So he did not wish to speak much of life with his family. It made me all the more curious, and I began to devise ways to ask more about them, though I knew I should not.

Finally, he asked, "Where were you walking?"

I would allow him to escape the topic. For now.

"Up the hill. It is my favourite spot. When I reach the top and look back, it reminds me how insignificant we are."

He looked to the treetops with narrowed eyes, then

recited, "'For I have learnt to look on nature, not as in the hour of thoughtless youth, but hearing oftentimes the still, sad music of humanity'." He paused and looked at me. "Wordsworth. Do you know his work?"

"I have read it, but I admit I am amazed you know it so well. I did not take you for a lover of poetry."

"Why?" he asked again, his brow furrowed.

"I... You seem serious."

"Much of poetry is serious," he said, his brow lowering into a full frown. "But am I as serious as that?"

I shrugged and began walking. He followed as I searched for words. "I do not know. You have an air of...of a man who thinks others are beneath him."

"They are," he answered quickly and a laugh burst from me before I could check myself. He blushed immediately. "I-I mean to say there are not many people who— well, of course, some— Dash it! That is exactly what I mean. It is a terrible character flaw, I know, but I cannot tolerate fools and I am not skilled sufficiently at pretending that I can."

I continued to laugh, and covered my mouth with my fingers, knowing I ought not to behave in such a fashion. Reassured when he smiled broadly at me, I confided, "*I find people both intolerable and fascinating. I want to know everyone's history.*" I huffed a little as the incline increased, leading us to the road where we would be appropriately in the view of any passers-by, which I thought safer than what might be perceived as hiding in the shadows. "The dairy man, the miller, the groom, the lord. I am infinitely curious to know how they live, what they dream of. When I speak to them individually, their stories fascinate me, yet when I observe people in a shop or at a dinner or an assembly and hear them speak, it is mostly utter nonsense. What most people share to impress others renders them intolerable."

"Yours is a more refined view. I do not ever find people fascinating. Certainly not the miller or the milliner, for that matter."

"I suppose you prefer speaking to lords and dukes?"

"Even less so!" He smiled again, and I noticed how straight his teeth were, save one off the centre that twisted just a charming touch. "Lords who are not inbred are so impressed with themselves that—" He stopped and turned to me. "Heavens! You have the power to make a person confess their every hidden thought."

I chuckled and continued to walk, so he followed. "It is a strange ability. Somehow others tell me their opinions and secrets. Not all, but many. Perhaps this is why I find them interesting."

We walked the last steps in silence, and when we reached the top, I pointed out some of the landmarks of Meryton, Longbourn, and the surrounding estates, including Haye-Park, telling bits of information about various tenants and landlords.

"You recall quite a bit."

"My mind is a busy place."

He offered a smile that only lifted the left side of his mouth, making my stomach kick. "Most women of your age and level of society are not great thinkers."

"Perhaps if they were given more to think about than ribbons and suitors, they would be more interesting."

"They, like you, have access to libraries, and yet none

come away knowing more than a fraction of what their tutors attempt to impart."

"What good would it do to know more? I find my knowledge frightens most gentlemen. And ladies."

"It does not frighten me."

When our eyes met, a vibration passed through me, the likes of which I had never felt. I wondered whether he felt something as well, since he looked immediately away, appearing to study the church in the distance.

Silence dragged on until I broke it. "My only purpose in life is to find a husband. Or so my mother says again and again. I try to hold in my thoughts, but I cannot. Nor can I force my face to behave, so it reveals the truth."

He turned back. "Truth is underrated."

"And what is your truth?"

He chewed on his lower lip. "That I ought not to say what I am thinking."

I threw my hands in the air in mock exasperation. "And truth floats away like cold breath in the night!"

"You are a poet."

I shook my head and then stopped when I saw a shift in his face. All mirth was gone. Instead, it was what I could only call longing. My heart pounded as I studied his lovely face. Thick brows, straight nose, lips neither too thick nor too thin.

Just above a whisper, I said, "Tell me. Tell me the truth." My heart was now thrumming so hard it made my head spin.

He leant so close I could feel his heat upon my cheek. He smelled of soap and cinnamon, and his breath stirred the hairs on my brow, making me shiver.

"Are you cold?"

I shook my head and as I looked up, our lips touched. The moment was beyond imagination. Nothing, nothing in my life had ever felt so correct, so perfect.

He pulled back at once, looking dismayed. "Forgive me. I do not know what came over me."

My eyes drifted open as if I was waking from a sweet dream, but when I saw his furrowed brow and drawn mouth, I was alert at once. "That was my first kiss and—"

"Your first— Blast." He turned and said to the ground, "A first kiss."

"Was—Was it bad?"

"No. Of course, no." His eyes met mine. "But I felt—" His brows drew closer together, his face suffused with shock. "I have never felt that way. As if I was...complete." Before I could share my astonishment at having had that exact thought, he added, "But I did not mean to take advantage of you."

"You did no such thing." I thought of how the world had narrowed to one spot, to the place where lips touched lips.

He straightened up and drew in a slow breath. "We ought to return you to your house."

"Let us not. At Longbourn there is my family and noise and distraction. Here it is only us and—"

"That is what I fear. This could be dangerous. Let us get to Longbourn." We walked a few paces side by side. "I must leave you. I do not trust myself." With that, he almost sprinted down the hill, leaving me in confusion. And awe.

CHAPTER 5

The rest of that day and evening, Mr Darcy sequestered himself with Mr Fitzwilliam, saying only that he needed to keep watch over his cousin. I suspected it was to put distance between us, though I dared tell no one. I suffered over it in silence, unable to eat or concentrate, bringing reprimands from not only Mama and Papa, but also Jane, who said I was worrying her. I desired to tell her what had occurred, but feared her response. My sister would keep my secret, of that I was certain, but making the details known to her still seemed perilous somehow. As I fell asleep that night, I resolved that it was to my benefit if Mr Darcy spent the rest of his stay in his cousin's room, for I did not trust myself if we were alone once again.

The next afternoon, however, Mr Darcy returned to Longbourn to visit with a nearly recovered Mr Fitzwilliam and joined us for tea. The sun shone brightly through the windows and the fresh air was calling me, which was good, as every time our eyes met, my stomach flipped in a most indelicate manner, and stopped my breath, which was highly inconvenient.

I leapt to my feet and declared that I simply had to walk.

"Lizzy," said my mother with unconcealed outrage. "We have guests!"

"One who is sick and another who needs no caretaking." I regretted my hasty answer the moment I said it, and felt compelled to look to Mr Darcy to see how he bore my impertinence. As soon as I looked at him, my legs went weak. But I was not some silly girl like my younger sisters. This could not stand.

I had almost escaped when Mr Darcy called after me, "Where are you walking today?" I froze and considered a lie, when he added, "I had thought to walk myself, though perhaps not to Meryton. I hear it is not much of a town." When I turned to face him, his eyes were sparkling, and he was barely containing a laugh at repeating our conversation from the day before.

Mama did not understand the joke, and her face twisted in offence. "Meryton might be small compared to *London*," she said with a tinge of bitterness in her voice, "but it is a fine town, I assure you."

"Perhaps Miss Elizabeth will show me that I might be persuaded."

My muscles tensed as all eyes turned to me. If I did not agree, it would be seen as very rude behaviour towards our guest. If I did agree, I would be spending the day with Mr Darcy, the most alluring man I had ever met who also made me lose my senses. More importantly, when last I saw Mr Darcy on my own, he was running away from me as fast as his feet would take him. What game was he playing?

"If you wait a few minutes and allow me to finish my tea, we can walk out together."

Lydia and Kitty were, of course, leaning their heads together, giggling at this spectacle, while my mother looked hopeful. Papa was immersed in his paper, only half aware that his daughter's reputation might be made or ruined in this moment.

I had to decide. There was no question. Yes, I would walk with him. "I shall change into my walking boots and then we might depart."

Jane stood. "Shall I accompany you?"

"Do not be silly!" my mother said, yanking her back to her seat. "They shall stay on the open road and all shall be well. Nothing to be concerned about, right my dear?" She cleared her throat, and when my father still did not respond, she yelled, "Mr Bennet!"

His head popped up and he comprehended that the room was looking at him. "Yes, dear."

We knew perfectly well that my father had, as often occurred, not heard the question, but Mama looked at Jane with triumph nevertheless. "Well, go on, then, Lizzy. Get your boots! Mustn't keep Mr Darcy waiting."

Mid-chew, Mr Darcy held up the better part of a roll in his hand as if toasting me. His wink before I left the room had me rushing to return.

An hour later, we were in the heart of Meryton. Though he claimed to be stuffed from breakfast, when we saw the window of Wright's filled with treats, Mr Darcy insisted we enter.

"Miss Elizabeth!" called out Mr Wright. "How good to see you!"

"How is Mrs Wright's hand?"

The baker leant on the counter and lowered his voice. "Improving, though she thinks not fast enough. I tell her that after slicing one's palm with a dough knife, it is a miracle she is recovering at all, but she is impatient."

"And Timmy?"

Mr Wright looked over his shoulder for the briefest moment, likely to ensure that his son was not about. "Struggling to get past the guilt."

"His mother's injury was not his fault," I said. "He dropped a sack of flour, which distracted her. It was not intentional."

Mr Wright sighed. "The boy has an overdeveloped conscience. He is working himself to the bone doing her work and his. I tell him it is not necessary, but he fears we will lose the shop if he does not."

"That cannot be true!"

He pressed his lips together for the briefest of moments, and I wondered whether that was an affirmation or a denial, or simply an indication that I had trodden too close to private matters. "So," he said, looking down at his baked goods, "what were you interested in purchasing today?"

I turned to Mr Darcy, who asked what was good. "Everything," I said. "If there is one wonder of Meryton, it is Mr Wright's delicacies."

"I have always had a weakness for marzipan."

"Wonderful choice," said Mr Wright. "And a jam tartlet for the lady?"

I nodded and Mr Darcy reached for his coins. Just then, Lydia and Kitty came through the door. "Lizzy! Lizzy!" cried Lydia. "We simply must have sweets this morning. Please!"

Kitty pushed her curled locks behind her shoulders and bounced on her toes. "Please, Lizzy."

"You both must have your allowances?"

Lydia ran her fingers along the display case, leaving marks, which I knew Mr Wright or one of his children would have to clean the moment my unruly sisters had departed. "We used it."

"On what?" I asked.

Both girls dissolved into giggles, and once recovered, Kitty said, "Ribbons. And sweets. And Lydia bought lace for a hat. And—"

"I shall treat you all," Mr Darcy said, interrupting either to silence them or to be generous. I was relieved either way, for they had their delicacies in hand and were scampering away moments later. Mr Darcy paid and we said our goodbyes, walking out onto the street.

"Do you not need to sit to eat the tartlet?" he asked.

I felt self-conscious, for I had been walking while unwrapping it as I always did. I wondered what I would do if the jam dripped on my bodice as sometimes occurred, but chose to be my truest self. I shook my head, hoping all would go well.

He bit into the marzipan. Little flecks of sugar snowed down upon his coat, but he did not seem to notice or care, for his eyes were closed as he lost himself in the pleasure of the taste. Then he opened his eyes and looked down, chuckling while brushing at his clothing. "You know the people of your town well, and are not hesitant to speak to all." He took another bite, this time leaning forwards in an attempt to keep his clothes neater.

"Why should I be? They were born into different circumstances, but an accident of birth does not make me superior."

"Many would disagree with you."

"Perhaps, but they would be wrong."

He laughed so hard he sprayed marzipan into the air, making him laugh even harder. He covered his mouth, face red with embarrassment, and apologised, but I assured him through my own laughter that all was well. He reached out to wipe a bit from my bodice, but caught himself before he touched my chest, and I removed the crumb myself. A moment later, he asked, "Are you always so assured?"

"A good question."

We walked past the shop that sold fripperies, where Lydia and Kitty were making their presences known, and I steered us towards a bench facing the stream.

"You have not yet answered."

I looked out to the pastures and stone walls stretching into the distance. "I know what I believe and have a sense of things."

"Many would not share their thoughts so openly."

"I do not understand hiding one's beliefs. What is there to fear?"

His face grew dark, and he looked up to the hill where we walked yesterday. "There can be repercussions for honesty. And for being oneself."

It seemed there was more to this but as he did not

offer, I did not press him, instead asking if he would like to continue walking.

"Let us return to Longbourn." Before my profound disappointment at an outing cut short could fully blossom, he added, "We need not rush. I would prefer the woods to town, if that would be agreeable, as too much time in London has made me weary of commerce and crowds."

I did not think Meryton was especially crowded, though the thought of more time together, as well as privacy, sounded both dangerous and divine. I led us on the road towards home and then veered into the dappled light of tree cover.

"Have you always had an appreciation of nature?" I asked.

He nodded. "The park at Pemberley is ten miles around, and there are acres of woods and fields beyond that, so there was plenty to explore. And I preferred to be away from the house, so the woods became my refuge."

"Why is that?"

Discomfort flashed across his face but he kept walking another few steps before stopping short. I had a sudden fear that, being alone as we were, he might kiss me again. I fancied he looked like he might wish it, but no such thing occurred. Instead, he merely studied my every feature and I did the same.

How could a person be as handsome as this? How could someone so striking have his features marred with flickers of self-doubt and discomfort?

He smiled. "You are a lovely creature, Miss Elizabeth, and I find I wish to tell you everything."

"Then do."

"I like you. Very much."

I hoped he would say more, but he hesitated.

"I never thought I would find someone I like as well as you," I said, feeling a little shy. "You are perfect."

His body stiffened and an expression of anger swept across his face. "I am hardly perfect."

"Forgive me if I have spoken amiss."

He did not look at me for a moment. "I... There has always been an expectation of perfection in my family." His fists were clenched, his shoulders high. It was the most shocking transformation from the man who had been enjoying marzipan not half an hour earlier. "I have tried to live up to what they want, but it is never enough. The family. I am—" He clutched his waistcoat as if it were the offending part of his life. "I am not free. I wish to be anyone but a Fitzwilliam or a Darcy, and I am shackled by being both."

I blinked a few times as he worked to steady his breath. "Your family and who they are need not define you and who you are," I said quietly.

"But they do." He took my hand, bent, and placed a kiss upon it, his eyes meeting mine as he straightened. It seemed there was a great deal said in the silence between us which stretched and lengthened for an eternity until he said, "We ought to return to the house."

"You do not wish to run from me as you did yesterday?"

His lips quirked into a begrudging smile. "How is a young woman such as yourself not accosted at every turn by all of the gentlemen about?"

"It would seem, sir," I said, laying my hand in the

crook of his arm, "that you are the only one to apprehend the fullness of my charms."

"Then the men here are utterly witless."

I laughed, as did he. "None have the resources to make an agreement attractive to my family." As we walked on, I explained my father's entailment, and about the financial losses that had resulted in making my sisters' and my marriage prospects all the more urgent.

"Money and power," he said, then sighed. "What a shame that we cannot disregard them."

Did he mean that as a general statement or in regards to forming a connexion with me? I dared not ask.

We were approaching a clearing so near the edge of the woods that we could see Longbourn but not be seen ourselves. It had been a favourite retreat of mine since I was a girl.

He paused. "Could we remain here for a bit? I think I am not yet ready to face your entire family."

I was sorry not to know the answer to my unasked question but wordlessly agreed to the change in subject. "They are rather overwhelming at times." I sat upon a boulder and he sat beside me. "Do you think Mr Fitzwilliam needs you?"

"I suspect he is being well looked after."

I smiled at that. "Tell me more of Scotland."

We passed much of the afternoon this way, with a pleasant combination of conversation and moments that almost led to a repeat of our near-scandalous actions the day prior. If only such perfection could last.

Late the next morning, we met once again in the clearing, though this time, our approach was more clandestine, he journeying straight from Haye-Park to the woods, so as to avoid comment by my mother or sisters.

The day was fine and warm but even so, we found ourselves sitting close together on the grass. He cut a slice of apple and I took it, enjoying the sweetness. As we shared stories, I noted he was generous and steady and strong and fascinating and kind, and I thought I would like to spend forever with this man. I hoped he felt the same, but dared not speak such words.

As the shadows lengthened, I asked, "When you return from your travels, what will you do?"

"Begin training as a barrister, I suppose."

"Every time you speak of your future profession, you sound indifferent."

"I feel indifferent." He leant back, looking up at the sky. "There are few options for me. I have no interest in the clergy, which, as a second son, seems to be what is expected."

"And the military? Your cousin seems proud of his upcoming position."

"My cousin does not despise the idea of following rules or of marching in formations as I do. I bristle at confinement. Worse, when I mention that killing others is a vital part of a soldier's life, he is unbothered and dismisses my concerns outright. Even if I desired to be a soldier, my family would never accept it." He groaned.

"Do you need a profession?"

"I need a way to pass my days beyond attending hunting parties and balls."

"Can you do nothing else?"

He sat up on one elbow. "What do you propose? Shall I make hats? Open a pastry shop?"

"I should think your love of marzipan might prove useful." I bit back a smile, attempting to appear solemn, and was pleased when my advice prompted him to smile before he replied.

"Your lack of care for what is expected is both absurd and charming. There are limitations to what I do. And who I..."

"Who you what?"

"Love."

He breathed once, twice. Another time. Was he going to propose? And if he was, what would I say? Yes. Yes!

"I want—"

I heard a sudden clattering coming down the road.

We turned our heads. The noise grew louder. Taking my hand, he pulled us closer to the edge of the woods, still staying far enough in the shadows that no one would know we were there. Approaching was a black lacquered coach with deep brown spokes pulled by six magnificent horses. Strong, regal, heads held high. The thought came that the horses were like Mr Darcy, and I nearly laughed.

"Mr Goulding," we said simultaneously.

CHAPTER 6

Mr William Goulding had sent word to my parents that he would collect Mr Fitzwilliam, and they had invited him to come for tea.

Mr Darcy offered me a sheepish smile. "Is it two o'clock already? Once in your presence, I lose myself."

"We should not arrive at the house together."

He straightened his waistcoat with a wink, and walked through the woods to approach the house another way.

As I entered the drawing room, my father was greeting Mr Goulding. Mama gestured for Mary to stand up straighter, but the attention had the opposite effect. My youngest sisters giggled, which made Mary scowl. Mr Fitzwilliam was sitting on the sofa looking healthier, but remained seated with a blanket draped over his shoulders.

I tripped on the edge of the carpet as I approached, but not so much that I splayed out upon the floor. It did, however, attract the attention of all gathered.

"Miss Elizabeth," said Mr Goulding with a bow, "how

wonderful to see you again. I assume your headache from the night of the assembly has passed."

"Indeed. I am sorry we did not get to speak—"

"Or dance!" he said. "As I recall, you are a competent dance partner."

"More than competent," my mother said with a huff.

Mr Goulding had always been one to tease. His easy manners confused Mama at times, for she was never certain when he was making a good-natured joke and when he was laughing at a situation. He was good-looking, but too aware of it for my taste, and too interested in horses and gambling, and not enough about books and the inner lives of others to ever be of true interest to me, even if my financial inferiority had not been an impediment. He had always been passable as a dance partner at an assembly if one could tolerate the lack of variety in subjects.

Mr Darcy entered and the men greeted each other warmly. I curtseyed, and when I looked at Mr Darcy, my heart sank. Mama's gaze lingered on his dirty boots and on my equally dirty hem.

I said, "I was walking."

"She walks constantly," Mr Darcy said, a nervous edge to his voice.

The corners of Mr Goulding's lips twitched, and I thought he might be hiding a smile. What had Mr Darcy told him of his walks? "Yes, Miss Elizabeth has often been found treading through the woods about these lands."

"A very healthy habit," Mr Darcy said.

His discomfort seemed to amuse Mr Goulding. "Indeed."

We were saved further awkwardness by Hill hastening in with pots of tea, followed by Bridget, who carried trays of small sandwiches and cakes.

"Darcy and I shall take Fitz to Haye-Park after tea. It is certainly a more appropriate place for a night's rest than the inns you seem to prefer, Darcy."

Mr Darcy said, "I like inns because they are populated by common folk."

"Common folk. Who needs the riff-raff? You have more money than nearly anyone in the country, and—"

"My *family* does, and I think it best not to discuss such things."

"Our house is not as grand as Haye-Park," said Mama, "but Mr Fitzwilliam could use another day's rest, I suspect." Her eyes darted between Jane and Mr Fitzwilliam, which caused them to look away from one another, though I did notice he looked back at her not a moment later. Mr Fitzwilliam coughed, and Jane asked how he was feeling.

My mother asked, "Some entertainment?" She looked at Jane, who hated to be on display and was already blushing at the thought.

Mr Darcy said, "I understand that Miss Elizabeth plays beautifully."

When our eyes met, I felt the familiar flip of my stomach.

I feared what Mr Goulding might say about our pianoforte and my skill, and so was looking for an excuse when Mary sprang to her feet. "I shall play." Chin high, she flounced to the bench and sat upon it with a thud, causing the bench to screech upon the polished wooden floors and leaving a scratch. Her playing was, as always, competent but leaden. Her voice was not terrible, but she had little facility for Italian, making me wish she had chosen a different tune. Mr Goulding and Mr Darcy looked at one another repeatedly, and I even caught Mr Goulding flinch at a particularly egregious error of pronunciation. Lydia and Kitty giggled, ignoring our father's throat clearing, meant to be a warning but was far too subtle.

When the song came to a merciful close, Mary announced she would sing another.

I flashed my father an imploring glance, but he was already on his feet, clapping and suggesting she give someone else an opportunity.

Before anyone could accept or decline, Mr Goulding had risen. "We must get Fitzwilliam settled, but I thank you for your hospitality."

At that moment, a mouse scuttled past, sending Mama shrieking and Kitty and Lydia twittering as they tumbled over the back of the couch to get away. My father reached down and picked up the mouse by its tail, went to the window, opened it with one hand, and tossed it out the window. His casual air made it seem as if this was a regular occurrence in our home, though I could not remember a single rodent within Longbourn save for one when I was eight or nine.

"You have quite a talent for dealing with vermin, Mr Bennet." Mr Goulding spoke with what I feared was a sneer but might have been simple amusement. "I learn of new talents every time I visit Longbourn."

My insides roiled. What must the gentlemen think of our house and manners? My family's manners, save for

Jane's, were abominable. I had been ashamed by them before, but never so intensely. How could I steal Mr Darcy aside to— To what? Explain? Excuse? Promise I was nothing like them? No, there were no words.

As everyone filed into the hall, panic overtook me. I feared that the moment Mr Darcy stepped into the carriage, I would never see him again. Propriety dictated that I accept this and be still, but I could not.

"Mr Darcy," I said, and everyone turned. I hated the desperation in my voice and the pleading I knew was on my face, but could check neither. "Did you forget your hat?"

He stepped back into the parlour, feigning a search, as the rest exited the house.

I whispered, "Will I see you tomorrow?"

After a brief pause, he said quietly, "I am not certain."

My chest tightened.

"I... We ought not go on passing time together. I would not wish to lead you to...my family has expectations for me. I go where they say and act as they wish. I am to be austere and act proud and superior because that is what they model and it is what is expected. My cousin and I ran off on a whim, but that is over. Now, I must return to the life they expect me to lead. I must carry the Darcy name with pride and all that comes with it. I cannot run off with a girl simply because I love her desperately."

I gasped. "You do?"

He took my hand and nodded, pain twisting his features. "It does not matter that I do. Just as my cousin cannot marry your sister, for he needs an income and thus to marry into wealth, I cannot be with you for fear of shaming my family and losing all that I could have."

"Why would you shame your family?"

He tilted his head. "I will speak plainly. I cannot rejoice in the inferiority of your connexions, nor congratulate myself on the hope of relations whose condition in life is so decidedly beneath my own."

I blinked and blinked. "It is not as if you were unaware of my situation since the moment you walked into Longbourn."

"I thought I could look past it, but once Goulding arrived, I saw it all through his eyes and realised what my family would think. They are formidable, Miss Elizabeth. You have not met them, yet I assure you, they would make your life a misery. You have not met anyone such as the elder Darcys and their circle."

It was true. I did not know the varied ways the *ton* might reject and belittle me.

"We can speak more of this tomorrow. I need time to think, and Goulding is waiting."

My embarrassment turned into anger at his casual assumption that he could speak as he had and I would still wish to meet him. "After insulting me thus, you expect me to meet you tomorrow?"

He froze. "I hope you might. Meet me on the hill where we can see how insignificant we are."

He remembered my words.

He took my hand, and when he brought my knuckles to his lips, I noticed tears were brimming in his eyes. "Give me an evening to think."

I nodded, and he bowed and departed.

The following day, as I crested the hill where we had our first conversation, I was stunned to see Mr Darcy waiting. Part of me was certain he would break his word and run off without a proper farewell.

"You look pale," he said.

"I was upset. In truth, I cried most of last night."

His face crumpled. "No."

"Yes." His kind attention was too much to bear. "Mr Darcy, you wounded me."

His head drooped. "I know."

"Do you? I love my family, despite their faults, and could never be with a man who treats others harshly or thinks of those dearest to me with disdain."

"I was wrong to have spoken as I did. But I must explain that as we sat in your parlour, I could imagine my parents' reaction. They expect certain manners and behaviour and desires—desires that are not mine—and I feel crushed under these expectations."

"Why can you not be your own man?"

He shrugged. "I have never managed it. Whilst at Cambridge, I met many sorts of men and came to realise that I could strike out on my own, be different. I was attempting to do just that on my travels, but I will never not be a Darcy." My heart sank, as I assumed the conclusion was that he had decided this relationship could not progress, but then he added, "As I pondered my circumstance, I concluded that there is a benefit to being a second son. As long as I am not the head of the Darcy family, what need have I to follow their expectations?

They might disown me or limit my resources should I marry beneath me, but many men survive without large inheritances. I can do without. I wish to live the life I desire."

I heard then the sound of pounding hoofbeats approaching over the hill. A single rider was coming fast. We stepped off the road to make way, but as he approached, we realised it was Mr Fitzwilliam. As he drew nearer, he slowed the horse until he could dismount. I saw then that his face was ashen and sorrow was in his eyes.

"Darcy, come quick. It is your brother."

"Thomas? What about him?"

"He is—" Mr Fitzwilliam looked at me, swallowed hard and then looked back at his cousin. "An express has come. There was an accident."

A pause.

"H-He di— He is gone."

Mr Darcy stood completely still. "No," he whispered, his face slack. "It cannot be."

"It is. You are—"

Mr Darcy began to walk down the hill, hands at his sides as if in a dream, but his cousin pursued him.

"Darcy, you are next in line. You must return."

"No!" He spun around, pink blazing in his cheeks. "If I return, I will never be free!"

Mr Fitzwilliam took hold of his shoulder. "You must. It is your duty."

Mr Darcy stepped into his cousin and rested his head on Mr Fitzwilliam's shoulder, his body shaking. Mr Fitzwilliam stroked the back of his neck and said something so low I could not hear. After a few moments—long enough to watch a flock of birds pass overhead—Mr Darcy stood tall, wiped roughly at his face, and walked back up the hill to me.

"Miss Elizabeth, I must be away."

"I am so sorry about your brother." I reached out for him, but he pulled back beyond my reach. My heart plummeted. "Mr Darcy?"

He bowed and turned, mounting Mr Fitzwilliam's horse, and rode off without looking back.

Mr Fitzwilliam said, "I am sorry, as well, Miss Elizabeth. You would have made him very happy. And I would have liked to have spent more time with Miss Bennet. Alas, we all do as we are born to do."

He bowed and followed his cousin on foot, back to Haye-Park and directly out of my life.

CHAPTER 7

Spring 1811

An assembly was the last entertainment I desired for the evening. Jane insisted that I always felt this way. I had not disliked balls and assemblies while I was in London these past two years, but it was true here.

Two years! Yes, almost two years had flown by as I made new acquaintances and developed new friendships and new interests in London. I had discovered a passion for more than walks in the woods, which I did still adore, though they came with memories of Mr Darcy and the longing I still felt for him. Yet in London, there were museums and shops and streets filled with all manner of persons to observe and ponder. So many lives were being lived in a seemingly infinite number of ways.

And now I was back to the site of my heartbreak and frustrations. Meryton was too small. Too quiet. Too provincial. In the month since I had returned, I had done little but mope and wander. Two years away had done little to restore Longbourn to my good graces, and it was like being stabbed in the heart all day every day now that I was back.

The opportunity to live with the Gardiners had been a gift, and I would forever be grateful to my aunt and uncle for allowing me such a prolonged stay. My mother, despite the protests of her brother and his wife who said I could remain in perpetuity, had finally insisted I move home again. Her reasoning was not clear, but when was my mother's reasoning ever clear?

Why, *why* could I not accept my life as it was? Small assemblies would be my fate, as would a dull life. But did it have to be?

The assembly room was already hot when we arrived and full of familiar faces and one or two strangers as well. Jane and I were stopped every few steps, and I was greeted with surprise and welcome. I fixed a smile upon my face and answered all enquiries as politely as possible, though I ended conversations with as much haste as I could without being considered uncivil. My lack of desire for in-depth conversations seemed to surprise my neighbours, but I pretended not to notice that or the whispers after we moved on—some of which implied I thought myself too good for their company since spending time in town. I pushed the false smile higher.

At last, we walked to the refreshment table where I had spotted my oldest friend, Charlotte Lucas.

"Charlotte! You look lovely this evening."

She looked at her gown, a pale green, which I thought suited her complexion. "Mother had it made in hopes that

I might, at last, catch a husband, though I daresay it will take more than a dress for that to happen."

"Do not speak so harshly against yourself."

"If neither you nor Jane have secured a spouse, I have no chance," she said. "Lizzy, how did you find no one in London? There are far more men there than here." She sighed before sipping on her cup of negus.

Oh, if she only knew all that had transpired in London! I dared not share any of that with her as she would neither understand nor agree with my refusal of a proposal or my general views on marriage itself.

"Not too much of that," I said with a wink, knowing how quickly wine went to her head, "or you shall not be able to dance."

She tossed her head back and finished her cup, then filled another. "I have no cares in that regard. Far more women than men have appeared this evening. It is likely I shall never be asked."

At that very moment, her father approached with a man I had not seen before. Sir William introduced him as Mr Smith from Warwickshire; he wished to ask Charlotte to dance. Mr Smith was on the short side and decidedly plain, but his smile was warm and inviting. They moved towards the dance floor and waited for the next song to begin, chatting contentedly all the while. It made me happy to see, for Charlotte's fears of becoming a spinster were well founded. Her father had some fortune, but prospects for her had proved slim, as his holdings were neither enough to entice a gentleman of means, nor so little she could marry a man who needed his profession.

Settling for a merchant would be a disappointment for her father who had worked up to his station.

"Lizzy?" Jane murmured into my ear. "It has been weeks and you have yet to tell me why you refused Mr Corbet."

"Not here," I said. *Not ever*, I thought. Mr Corbet, a sweet-natured man I had met in town, would make some lady a perfectly agreeable husband; alas, that lady could not be me. Why tell Jane yet again why no man would do? No man after Mr Darcy, that is. No one was as mesmerising, and those I danced with had created neither spark nor the discovery of a missing piece. I could not force her to endure more of such tales.

"Girls," my mother said, approaching in a flutter, "why are you hiding by the refreshments? Go where the light is better so Jane's true beauty can be on full display."

Jane and I began laughing conspiratorially, and my mother was just opening her lips to rebuke us for our impertinence when a commotion at the door made us all turn our heads.

There *he* was.

My body felt robbed of its air and I thought I might melt into the ground. For a moment, I wondered whether my earlier thoughts of him had conjured him, for surely he could not really be present?

"Was not *that* the gentlemen who stayed with us so many years ago?" Mama asked, too loudly. "Mr Barcy, was it? Marcy?"

"Mr Darcy," I said, attempting not to tinge his name with poison. Or affection.

Jane's eyes locked on mine and I forced down all

emotion, trying my best to don a smile. It would not do to fall to pieces in front of a hundred friends and neighbours. When that did not work, I turned towards the window, hoping for a moment to gather my composure.

"Miss Bennet," a voice said. I turned back to see that Mr Coates, a gentleman who came to Meryton occasionally on his way to or from town, was bowing to Jane. "Might I have the pleasure of a dance?"

Jane looked to me and I nodded the slightest bit. She would desire to remain at my side, but that would not do, so I nudged her back for emphasis. After a brief hesitation, she agreed and they departed. Mama clapped and went to tell Lady Lucas of her daughter's triumph, forgetting that Charlotte had been asked to dance first. At least it left me to ease myself into the shadows of the room, seeking obscurity above all else as I moved about.

Without thinking, I wandered to the side where Mr Darcy's party stood. The young man with him was shorter than Mr Darcy. He had a pleasant countenance, and seemed to have easy, unaffected manners. He reminded me of, well, Mr Darcy—that is, the Mr Darcy I had met two years earlier. Certainly not the dour man whose eyes scanned the room and whose face was suffused with judgment and displeasure in all he beheld. One would never imagine that he knew at least some of these people, or that some had cared for his own cousin while he was ill.

From my place in the shadows, I heard that Mr Darcy's friend's name was Mr Bingley, and I watched as Mr Bingley became acquainted with some of the townspeople. He appeared to know Mr Coates, for their greeting was warm. It appeared Mr Darcy knew Mr Coates as well, though *his* nod to the man was curt. Mr Bingley's manner changed when Mr Coates introduced him to Jane; one could almost see the spark that went between them like a burst of lightning before the rain. Immediately, he asked her to dance, which Jane accepted with bashful delight, and they went towards the dancers, leaving Mr Darcy alone to skulk about the room. I remained where I was.

I managed to watch him without—I hoped—appearing to do so. His displeasure in the evening was apparent as he moved about the room speaking to no one, a dark, humourless cloud amid the frivolity. Eventually he came back to where his party had returned. The group included a Mr and Mrs Hurst as well as Mr Bingley's pretty sister, Miss Caroline Bingley, whose interest in Mr Darcy was plain. She continually touched his arm, and cocked her head, but he seemed impervious to her advances. He seemed impervious to everything, in fact.

Why did he come here? Why *here* of all places? Clearly it was not to see me. I overheard it said that his party had been at Netherfield Park—an estate that abutted Longbourn—for over a week, but he had not called at Longbourn. This was to be expected, however, for he could have called on me multiple times in London. My living there was no secret, but he never came near Gracechurch Street, at least as far as I knew.

And somehow, he did not appear at any gathering I attended in town—even the larger balls given by my aunt's more exalted friends. In the first months, I thought it was a coincidence, or perhaps that his new duties as heir kept him occupied. Coincidence, however, can only last so long.

Mr Bingley had finished his dance with Jane but

appeared reluctant to give her up, standing and talking to her for some time. At length, he returned to where Mr Darcy stood, alone again as Miss Bingley had been reluctantly taken off to dance and Mr and Mrs Hurst had wandered off somewhere. "Come, Darcy, I must have you dance. I hate to see you standing about by yourself in this stupid manner. You had much better dance."

"I certainly shall not. You know how I detest it unless I am particularly acquainted with my partner."

Had I known this fact? In the days we were acquainted, dancing had not been a topic of discussion. Days. Days! It had been mere days we were together more than two years earlier, but they had left such an impression that my life had been forever altered. And something had altered *him* for the worse since then. Was it more than the death of his brother? Had becoming the eldest son, the heir to a grand estate and its duties and responsibilities, destroyed his sweet spirit and turned him arrogant and grim? It made me sad to think on it—both his loss and the possibility that all his goodness had been quashed. But perhaps that was not so. Outside of those days we had spent together in Meryton, had he always been so dour? Was this the real man?

Mr Darcy frowned severely as he continued his disgust-filled speech. "At such an assembly as this, it would be insupportable. Your sisters are engaged, and there is not another woman in the room whom it would not be a punishment to me to stand up with."

Had he seen me? If he had, would he have approached? Why would he? Would he consider it a punishment to stand up with *me*?

"I would not be so fastidious as you are for a kingdom," cried Bingley. "Upon my honour, I never met with so many pleasant girls in my life as I have this evening, and there are several of them you see uncommonly pretty."

"*You* are dancing with the only handsome girl in the room," said Mr Darcy.

Did he remember Jane's fancy for his cousin? Did he remember sitting with us in our parlour? Did he remember the woods or our kiss on the hill? Of course, he would have to, and yet he was not indicating such a connexion to his friend.

"Oh! she is the most beautiful creature I ever beheld! But there is one of her sisters sitting down just behind you, who is very pretty."

"Which do you mean?" To my astonishment, he turned and our eyes met. Quickly he withdrew his gaze. Loud enough for me to hear, he said, "She is tolerable; but not handsome enough to tempt *me*; and I am in no humour at present to give consequence to young ladies who are slighted by other men. You had better return to your partner and enjoy her smiles, for you are wasting your time with me."

Had anyone else made such a comment, I would have marched off and told the story with great spirit among my friends as I delighted in anything ridiculous. However, this did not feel ridiculous. This felt personal and it wounded me to my core.

Doing my best to disguise my pain as hauteur, speaking not a word, I brushed past him and marched straight to Jane, telling her I felt ill and would walk home.

"Alone? No Lizzy, you cannot."

"I cannot stay, Jane, and it is scarcely a mile, a mile I have walked hundreds of times in my life."

She let me slip out, and I was glad that she would remain, hoping she might dance another with Mr Bingley. I, however, planned to pack my trunks and go straight back to my aunt and uncle in London.

CHAPTER 8

"So, he saw you and said such a horrible thing?" My friend, Miss Phoebe Festing, was suitably aghast at Mr Darcy's behaviour towards me.

"You would not have believed the alteration in his character." I sipped my tea, relieved to be back in my friend's parlour in London with its tall windows, pale gold drapes and soothing robin's egg blue walls that offset the cream and gold furnishings. From the moment I sat here upon my first arrival to London, I had always felt at home. I had been introduced to the Festing family by my aunt, who had been friends with Mrs Festing since they were girls. Miss Festing had become a fast friend to me, and she and I had spent countless hours in this room. We had admired our reflections in the gold-framed mirrors, laughed at the grave faces in the many portraits that festooned the walls, and had run our toes along the luxurious carpet—without our stockings on one daring occasion. We had spent hours staring at the intricate patterns on the ceiling, tracing them with our fingers in the air and practising our drawing by recreating its lines on our papers. It was one place I truly felt myself.

Mrs Festing had entered the room. "Whose character do you speak of?"

"Mr Darcy's, ma'am."

"Oh, him again." She frowned, and sat on her cream and gold settee.

"Mother, she *saw* him, for the first time in years. This is a new development."

Mrs Festing cocked her head at me. "And what, pray tell, was so altered about him?"

"Everything," I said. "I would not have recognised him as the same person. He was rude, aloof, and excessively serious, particularly given that we were at an assembly."

"Perhaps the death of his parents has hardened him," suggested Mrs Festing.

"Death of his—? When?"

"I cannot recall exactly, but more than a year ago, I think. I heard talk of it. There was a carriage accident during a storm. I do not know any details, but I had not connected that news with the gentleman you had spoken of, and so did not think to tell you of it. Our circle does not associate with theirs, so it was mere gossip as far as I was concerned."

I sat surprised and sorry that I had not known, for I might have extended a kind word to him at the assembly, no matter how wretched his behaviour towards me.

Miss Festing took my hand. "Perhaps that unhappiness explains his attitude towards you."

Mrs Festing shook her head. "Girls, I believe too much thought about a man is unhealthy."

Mama would disagree with her, which is why I preferred Mrs Festing on such occasions.

It had been nearly impossible to get my mother to agree to let me return to London, but I suppose she saw there was no choice. By the time the others had returned from the assembly, I had packed my trunks. Mama said it would be impolite to arrive at Gracechurch Street without any forewarning, but I did not care. She threatened not to give me the funds for travel, but I said I should be happy to walk. At last my father took me into his study to discuss the matter; when I dissolved into tears and said I could no longer tolerate the provinciality of Meryton, he agreed to let me go. I could see my words hurt him, for he loved Hertfordshire and Longbourn, and likely took my dissatisfaction as an offence. I assured him that my love for the family was in no way diminished, and that I would, in time, likely come to appreciate my home.

He had taken my hands and said, "If you had already found a husband, you would have left me anyway, my dear Lizzy. My only desire is your happiness."

"I propose an outing," said Miss Festing, recalling me to the present. "A lecture or a museum, perhaps?"

And this was why I so loved being in town: endless ways to fill our days, each more stimulating to the mind than the next.

"Such a shame the Leverian Museum closed," said Mrs Festing. "You were fascinated by the cases of shells when you were younger."

"Yes, Mother, but the antlers and stuffed beasts sent me running."

"You always were so squeamish."

"Oh!" Miss Festing leapt to her feet, dramatic even by her excitable standards. "Let us go to the Egyptian Hall!"

"Let's do," said Mrs Festing with a warm smile, and I agreed to whatever adventure we were about to have, as the Festings rarely led me astray.

As we gathered our pelisses and hats, Miss Festing's young brother Richard was sent for.

While we waited, she asked me, "Have you heard of William Bullock?" When I shook my head, she said, "He is a naturalist. He made his fortune in jewellery and built the Egyptian Hall to display his collection of oddities."

Richard dashed down the steps and nearly barrelled into his mother.

"Heavens, young man!" she said. "Calm yourself."

"I want to see the shrunken heads!"

Miss Festing took hold of his askew collar and pulled it into place. "I do not believe they have shrunken heads at the Egyptian Hall, but they have other excitement."

"Matthew said there were heads!"

"Well then, we shall have to check for ourselves." Mrs Festing took his hand and marched out the door with the eager young lad in tow.

———

I was amazed by the hieroglyphs decorating the Egyptian Hall. I told my companions that I wished I could translate them to know what the builders were attempting to communicate. Mrs Festing said she suspected they were nonsensical, but Miss Festing whispered that perhaps they were naughty, which sent us into a fit of giggles.

The room was full of stuffed exotic animals. Richard ran towards them and Mrs Festing gave chase. Remembering their story from earlier, I asked my friend if she wished to go to another room.

Looking up at the elephant, its glass eyes were so realistic I expected the trunk to swing any moment. "I am no longer a child, so I shall not run screaming from the place," said Miss Festing. She stepped to the next animal —a rhinoceros whose horn made me shiver. "While I am no fan of this art form, for it makes me melancholy, I can appreciate the opportunity to see these beasts. Another day we could go to the Tower to see the Royal Menagerie again. I do love the lionesses."

Richard was still staring at the animals but Miss Festing and I asked her mother if we might continue on. We next entered a room full of artifacts from Captain Cook's travels abroad, gazing at the objects and reading the signs to learn more. Oh to see such places!

"I wish I could be an explorer!" said Miss Festing, looping her arm through mine and bringing me to the next room. "To travel the world and meet different sorts of people would be thrilling."

"I agree, though Captain Cook *was* killed over a dispute with the local people on one of the islands."

"I suspect you and I would be more diplomatic than most men. The way they throw their power around and threaten and take things can only upset people."

"What these explorers need is a woman. We are far better equipped in the art of diplomacy. How else could we survive?"

"Women as diplomats?" A man's voice behind us made us turn. "I never would have known."

"Mr Lambert!" Miss Festing exclaimed, her face like the sun coming from behind a cloud. "May I present my friend, Mr Peter Lambert, to you? Mr Lambert, this is Miss Elizabeth Bennet."

He bowed his head, his eyes lingering a moment on my face before turning to Miss Festing again. "It is marvellous to see you. Are you with your family?"

"Yes. My mother and Richard are somewhere hereabouts. We left them with the stuffed beasts."

"You never *did* like such displays."

Miss Festing chuckled. "You remember."

"Of course. You ran screaming from the great hall at my family home when you saw the—"

"Wild boar on the wall!" they finished together, laughing.

Miss Festing turned to me. "Unfortunately, Mr Lambert's father is an enthusiastic hunter, and the stuffed carcasses are strewn everywhere."

Mr Lambert barked out a laugh. "Strewn? You make it sound as if carcasses were simply left to rot on the sideboard and on the carpets." When she merely shrugged and offered a coquettish smile, he told me, "Stuffed and displayed. She might not have liked it but it *is* tasteful."

"If tasteful is glass eyes pushed into the cadavers of magnificent beasts and put on display," Miss Festing replied playfully.

He threw up his arms in equally good-natured surrender. "I shall never win this argument. I suggest we move on to a new room to explore the treasures."

"I do not recall inviting you to join us," she teased.

He tucked his lips between his teeth evidently to keep himself from laughing and leant in. "Your grandmother would reprimand you for such impertinence."

She whispered, "Then it is a good thing she is no longer alive."

The laugh he emitted turned heads and he cleared his throat to control it, then escorted us to the next exhibit hall. At first, the room was appealing, but alas, as we moved onward, there was a display of an enormous serpent, shown coiled up and eating a finely dressed woman. This was no mild depiction, but bloody and gruesome, with lacerations and ripped flesh abounding.

Miss Festing beheld it for scarcely a second before uttering a quiet scream and falling into a swoon. I had never known her to faint, and if not for Mr Lambert being so near and my already having an arm on her, she would have fallen to the ground.

He and I helped her out the door and to a bench. As I fanned her face and whispered kindnesses to her, Mr Lambert, red-faced, grumbled, "Why is there no warning on that room? How could they be so irresponsible as to exhibit such a spectacle that ladies might see?"

Although I had seen many ladies fascinated by the serpent, I chose not to correct him. "Perhaps you might find her mother for us?"

He agreed and left me with Miss Festing, who was now sniffing softly into her gloved hands. "What an embarrassment to cry like this in public. And to swoon. I actually swooned!"

"You did," I said. "It was so lady-like I hardly recognised you."

She chuckled weakly and took the handkerchief that I offered to her. A moment later, Mrs Festing hurried towards us, her face pale with concern.

"I am well. I was womanish and had a fit."

"Fainting is not a fit," her mother corrected. "Come, let us return home."

"That is not fair!" Richard crossed his arms across his chest. "I wish to see the rest of the exhibits!"

A quiet argument ensued before Mr Lambert kindly offered that he remain with the boy. I was charmed by his solicitude and glanced at my friend, wondering at the nature of their attachment. They had seemed merely friendly to me so far but perhaps it was something more.

Mrs Festing said. "If you are certain?"

He nodded and our parties separated.

CHAPTER 9

When I returned to the Festings' house the following day, Mr Lambert was already there. We sat and chatted and ate and drank tea, and when I declared it was time for me to return home, he offered to accompany me.

"My aunt has sent her maid with me," I told him. "She is below stairs."

"Nevertheless," he said, and stood.

Mrs Festing's smile was too eager but Miss Festing's faltered. That dimming of her joy gave me pause, but it seemed as if the wheels of this scheme had been set into motion, so I agreed.

I wrapped my shawl around my shoulders at the door. "Mr Lambert—"

"You may call me simply Lambert if you prefer. All of my friends do."

I hesitated, wondering whether I was a friend. The look on Miss Festing's face popped into my mind. She had never spoken of Mr Lambert romantically. I could not recall any admissions or even any insinuation that she fancied anyone—so was I meant to deny myself a closer acquaintance? I did not believe so. Nevertheless, I would not get carried away with Mr Lambert before asking Miss Festing about the nature of her true feelings.

We spoke amiably along the short distance to my aunt and uncle's, commenting on the loveliness of the day and pausing to pet a dog whose owner shared the same long face and flopping mane of hair. We stopped at the bottom of the front step at Gracechurch Street, where one of the Gardiner's housemaids was passing by with a basket. She carefully averted her eyes but offered a small smile and I asked, "Judith, how is your cough today?"

Her step hitched and her eyes darted to Mr Lambert then back to me. "Much better, Miss." She looked at him once more and scurried away towards the servants' entrance around the back.

"You speak to servants in such a familiar fashion?"

"I do."

He cocked his head and nodded but said nothing more of it. He regarded the house. "Do you enjoy living here?"

"Yes. Being in town is ever so much more exciting than Meryton."

"Why do your parents not have a house here? Do they take one for the Season?"

I could be honest and tell the entire truth by sharing that we have not the funds for such a venture, but that was likely too much to share on so short an acquaintance. "Neither of my parents particularly enjoy it here."

"I can imagine the bustle of town can be off-putting."

"Or thrilling," I replied with a smile. "But they do not see it as I do."

"What has been your favourite thing about London?"

"Every day there is something new to see or do. Probably the best thing, however, has been meeting the Festings. Miss Festing is a wonderful friend and exciting adventurer—as long as there are no dead animals involved."

"Yes, she is sensitive." He paused, staring into the distance. "Your friendship with Miss Festing is, in fact, something I wished to enquire about. As her friend, you likely know her mind."

I hoped he would not ask whether she would be hurt by his attentions to me. "I do in many things."

"Do you think she might object to a nearer acquaintance with me?" His cheeks took on a ruddy hue as he added, "That is to say a...more of a romantic leaning?"

It was she he cared for. What a happy relief. "I do not believe she would have any objection to that."

He bent to pet another passing dog, making me wonder how he ever made it to his destinations given the number of canines in the city. "She is headstrong and independent—two qualities I admire in her—and she has never given any indication that she was looking for a husband."

"Even the most independent of us are in want of husbands."

"Is that so?" He cocked his head and looked at me a moment, seeming relieved to have gotten the delicate part of his own speech over with. "Even you, Miss Bennet?"

"Even me," I acknowledged.

"Would you like an introduction to some of my eligible friends?"

I thought to refuse, but considered my mother. "If you have a desirable bachelor friend or two somewhere, I would not object to making his acquaintance."

The next morning when I arrived at the Festings, Mr Lambert was again already there. The same was true the next day and the third. Though I wanted to be happy for Miss Festing, I was envious of the time they were now spending with one another. Not wishing to interfere, on the fourth morning, I set out without plans to call on my friend, taking only my aunt's maid for a companion. Sarah was a sweet girl but determinedly mindful of her station, answering in the fewest syllables possible whenever I asked her a question, so eventually we fell silent.

We passed the boot makers, the clock-masters, paper-stainers, and the linen drapers. Cheapside might not have been as fashionable as Bond Street but certainly had everything a person could desire, save for the opportunity to meet other persons of fashion.

Deciding I would treat myself to some fine paper for letters to my family, I entered the stationers and chose a lovely pale-yellow paper that reminded me of the sun shining on Longbourn. Satisfied with my purchase, I stopped on the next block down to buy a tartlet for myself and a sweet roll for Sarah, and decided to go to the grounds of St Paul's Cathedral to eat and consider what I might write. As I had no ink or quill or a surface on which to write, contemplation of my words would have to do for now. I handed my parcel to Sarah and strolled along, enjoying the clear day.

Sarah sat on a bench near the churchyard entrance and I settled on another ensconced in the garden. As I ate my tartlet, and pondered to whom I would write first, I noticed a long queue at a side entrance to the cathedral. There were men of varied ages, heads down, shuffling forward. I suspected the line was for alms or a warm meal, and regarded my tartlet with thankfulness and a touch of guilt.

A young man strolled past me, his eyes fixed on the line. He sat on the next bench, continuing to stare at them. He shook his head, rose, walked a few brisk steps towards the men, spun around and sat back down with a huff. He rose once more but sat again. It was riveting. His head twitched towards me and our eyes met.

I had been caught staring shamelessly and felt I ought to say something, though I was hardly in the habit of addressing men with whom I had no prior acquaintance. Placing the remainder of my tartlet on a cloth in my lap, I said, "Excuse me but you seem distressed, sir. Might I be of assistance?"

He paused for a moment before replying. "That queue is the source of my dismay. Those men are in need of charity because our society does not support its people. They suffer endlessly with little or no hope of overcoming their debts. Too many are in servitude and countless more are starving or in housing that is shameful."

It was remarkable to hear someone speak so. No one I knew spoke so freely and passionately about issues regarding the poor, though it was a subject that weighed on my mind often. The poor were a fact of life. Whenever I mentioned any concerns to family and friends, my comments were treated with distaste and I was assured that we did what we could by continuing to care for our own tenants and people at Longbourn Village.

"By your silence I infer that I have shocked you," the man said. "I do apologise."

"You have not shocked me," I said, noticing his hair was in need of a cut, as the waves of brown flopped and flowed more than was fashionable. "I too was watching the line before your arrival. It grieves me to see so many in need."

"Sorrow is natural, but what will you *do* with that emotion?"

"I beg your pardon?"

"You clearly have the means to do something to help others," he said, gesturing towards the remaining bit of tartlet, "so what shall you do?"

I felt heat rise in my cheeks. "And what do *you* do other than storm about in churchyards and plague young ladies eating tartlets?"

A smile played at his lips. "It is a conundrum. I am moved yet rendered powerless by expectation."

"Whose expectations are those?" I asked him, wishing to take another bite of my pastry and yet feeling the awkwardness in so doing.

"My family's."

"Ah yes, family expectations." I thought of Mr Darcy, of my sisters, of my aunts and uncles and friends. "Every man and woman I know is stymied by expectation. It tempers our moods, guides our decisions, dictates our marriage prospects, our friendships, who we dance with and for how long. It is exhausting."

"Your thoughts reflect mine perfectly."

Why was I speaking so openly and at such length to a complete stranger? Perhaps because he was a stranger. But also, there was something about him that drew me in. His searching eyes? His passion? I was not certain. I turned my head to see whether Sarah was paying attention. She was near, but staring at the tops of the trees.

I asked, "What is the nature of your family's expectation of you?"

He tugged at his coat, which was more rumpled and more worn than I would have expected given the expensive look and cut of the fabric. "I do not wish to go into the clergy, but I am a second son. That is what I am expected to do."

"You seem passionate about helping. Vicars help."

"Vicars are hypocrites," he said with a faint sniff.

I gasped.

He ran his fingers through his wild locks. "I apologise for shocking you again. You see, the men I know at Cambridge studying to enter the church are doing it not out of care but to stay amongst their wealthy friends and family. They were not called by God. It is merely a job to put food on the table and support the children they will inevitably have."

"Is it wrong to want to be comfortable?"

"It is when you are pretending to be holier, on a higher plane. They are not. They simply desire more sipping chocolate and coal to warm their beds than others can dream of."

"Oh dear! Do you disparage sipping chocolate, as well?" I bit my lip to hide a smile.

His eyes twinkled. "No, I love it. However..." He tugged at his collar. "It pains me to think that that is the only reason to speak God's words each Sunday."

I regarded my tartlet and wrapped it up again, no longer desiring to eat it. "Then why not become a barrister?"

"Thieves. Worse than the clergy."

"Sir, I begin to wonder if there is any occupation you find worthy of a man," I said with a faint smile to show I was at least partly teasing.

He looked almost fierce as he said, "Men who work with their hands."

"Then become a builder or a tailor or work at the docks."

"My family would disown me completely," he said with a rueful chuckle. After a moment, he said, "I am Mr Owen Reeves."

I considered giving him a name not my own but relented within moments. "Miss Elizabeth Bennet." We each nodded in greeting.

After a few minutes of silence, he confided, "I am part of a group of men. We meet and talk, with the hopes of someday soon being in positions to make change."

"A worthy cause." I turned my head and saw Sarah now wandering near a bed of flowers. "I think often about servants. I want to know their names and what brought them into service or to a particular household. Others scoff at me, and the servants are initially suspicious when I ask them about themselves, but most lose their fear and tell me."

He leant forwards and I was struck by the expression in his hazel eyes and the fire behind them. "And what, Miss Bennet, have you learnt in these enquiries?"

"That most of their families sent them to work because they would have starved otherwise."

He studied me a moment. Something shifted in his face, though, not knowing him at all, I was not sure what it signified.

"Miss Bennet, did you know a child from the age of seven can be hanged for poaching a rabbit?"

I gasped.

"Or stealing lace. Or cutting down a tree."

"Seven?" A much younger Kitty came to mind, back when she was missing her two front teeth and tripped over her own feet. To imagine her on the gallows sent a shiver through me. "But do the authorities not consider *why* children would be stealing such things? Out of desperation, I suspect. A tree for firewood, or rabbits because they might be starving? Most children could not be criminal by nature."

"There are injustices beyond that. Miss Bennet, have you heard of frame-breaking?"

I nodded, for I had, indeed, read of workers who broke machines at factories. Those interviewed called themselves Luddites and said automation was destroying the working class. Many artisans who had spent years learning the crafts of weaving and other textile work were being replaced by various machines and untrained operators that could finish the work faster and cheaper. No one seemed to care which quality was better.

Mr Reeves continued, "But did you know framebreakers and protesters have been hanged or sent to Van Dieman's land?"

I gasped again.

"Hundreds have been killed or put on prison ships. Not just those destroying property."

"Heavens! What luck to have been born into such luxury, though I fear my comforts come at the expense of more than I realised."

I studied him for a moment, allowing me to appreciate his handsome face and feel some pull of attraction to him. Then he nodded just the slightest bit as if making a decision. "Miss Bennet, tomorrow there is a lecture at the Quaker Meeting House. A woman who has visited Newgate prison recently will be sharing tales of the horrors there. You ought to attend."

"I shall consider it, Mr Reeves." I rose, fearing too much time spent with this young man might leave an improper impression. "Thank you for the enlightening conversation."

He stood and bowed. "I shall hope to see you at our lecture then."

As Sarah and I left the churchyard, I felt certain that if I turned around, he would be watching. I did not turn around.

CHAPTER 10

The following afternoon, my aunt accompanied me to the Quaker Meeting House. When I first suggested it, she had refused, saying that while she appreciated that many were in need, the subject sounded too distressing. However, when I suggested I might go alone with only her maid, she said that would not do and consented to attend me.

Mr Reeves nodded from across the room when we entered. I nodded back, but made no attempt for further intercourse, knowing my aunt would not approve of my having spoken to a strange man in a park. Even so, I could not help but steal occasional glances at him. Despite his rumpled suit, well-made but uncared for—signalling that he came from a wealthy family but was working to deny or eschew it—he did cut a fine figure. Was he the sort of man to whom I could attach myself?

Mrs Fry was an arresting speaker, sharing stories from the women's prison that had my eyes brimming with tears. I had not known that children were in the prison cells with their mothers, their living conditions punishing and their resulting behaviour savage. She shared that, since prisoners had to pay for their own food and clothing, starvation was rampant. She told a particularly grim tale of women taking a gown from a dead baby to dress a living one. I was not the only audience member to cry out. The worst image—and one that gave me night terrors for days—was her description of young children clinging to their mothers as the women were dragged to the gallows. I wondered what happened to those little ones who had known such suffering. Did they return to the cells? Were they sent to foundling hospitals and orphanages? Would they be turned out onto the streets? There were ragged children who roamed about in small bands, but I merely avoided them. Never had I wondered deeply at their circumstances or thought to help.

As the hour ended, Mrs Fry asked for donations of money, clothes, and food, and to those connected with lawmakers, she asked them to use their influence to ask for change. I had no connexions of the kind that she spoke of, but I could certainly find the rest.

At the end of the lecture, I desired to remain and speak a moment with Mrs Fry, but my aunt said she ought to return home. Though I was disappointed, I did not argue and we departed.

"Aunt Gardiner," I said as we walked to the carriage, "was that not the most moving of lectures?"

"Moving? Yes. The most? I cannot say." She craned her neck, looking for her carriage.

"But are you not moved to act?" I asked earnestly. "The thought of all those children and what they must suffer!"

She looped her arm through mine. "Darling Lizzy, I act in the interest of my family and put my energies there. I do care for others, of course, but you will see when you are a wife and a mother that you shall not have the time to spend thinking of injustices in the same way."

The comment felt like a reprimand. I had come to town to meet a husband—or so I suspected she believed—and I was failing in this regard, though I cannot say I was really trying.

"Do you think we might ask for donations for the women of Newgate Prison when we call on some of your acquaintances tomorrow? We could—"

My aunt blanched and quickly interrupted me "No, we are not going to go house to house like beggars."

"But when your friends wish to raise funds for charity—"

"They hold an event of some sort. They do not go begging for donations. Elizabeth, I know you have not moved much in higher society but you must surely comprehend that there is a way these things are done." The silent implication was also that my mother had not taught me well enough, had not been a right example to me.

"Miss Bennet?"

I turned thinking Mr Reeves might have followed us. Instead, it was Mr Darcy.

I sucked in a breath, my surprise very nearly causing me to miss his request to be introduced to my aunt. Then, attempting to recover, I said, "Aunt Gardiner, may I present Mr Darcy? He went to Cambridge with Mr

William Goulding, our neighbour at Haye-Park, and we met when his cousin visited him some years ago."

"A pleasure to meet you, Mr Darcy," said my aunt, but her tone was strange. I had once told her of Mr Darcy's visit, though not of our kiss, or of his subsequent snubbing of me at the ball. I wondered what she recalled, and hoped she would not remark upon the latter.

"What brings you to town, Miss Bennet?" he asked. Though his jaw was set, making him look grave, he was still handsome.

"I am living with my aunt and uncle." I thought of how to explain without confessing that he was the reason I had twice run from Longbourn. Instead, I settled on the little joke we had once shared. "Meryton is not much of a town, after all."

He almost smiled, but made no further comment.

"Mr Darcy," I said, "I wish to offer you my condolences. I was greatly saddened to hear about your parents. And so close on the heels of your brother's passing. I cannot imagine—"

"Yes. A tragedy." He clenched his teeth, making it clear it was not a subject on which he cared to speak.

Aware of his discomfort, I softened my tone a little. "And amid so much sorrow, you have had a great deal of responsibility thrust upon you."

It worked; he relaxed the slightest bit. "Indeed I have. I am now responsible for all family lands and affairs. Tomorrow, I am returning to my sister in Derbyshire."

"She is much younger than you, if I recall."

Our eyes met and I thought I saw a flicker of recollection of our conversations in the woods where we spoke freely of our lives and hopes, but just as quickly, it was gone, replaced by as cold a stare as I had ever seen. "Indeed."

"Perhaps once you return, we shall meet again at a ball."

"I am afraid I have very little time for diversion these days. My duties are all consuming."

My aunt cleared her throat. I had nearly forgotten she was still holding my arm. "Lizzy, come. I see the carriage."

Mr Darcy bowed his head and I bobbed a curtsey. Obediently, I walked away with my aunt.

A few paces on, I turned back, hoping he was watching us depart. But he was gone.

CHAPTER 11

The next afternoon, my aunt had four ladies over for tea. As I sat listening to them speak of their children, my mind was once again returned to the horrors in Newgate. My new understanding of the dreadful hopelessness there seemed to be haunting my mind. Suddenly, I could not help myself; I began speaking of what I had learnt, leaving no detail unshared.

As I went on, relating what I had heard at the lecture, my aunt sent me a few looks and cleared her throat gently several times. Alas, I did not heed her quickly enough so she turned her attention away, conversing with her best friend and offering her guests the tray of sweets.

"Mrs Grant, have you tried these tartlets? I am vastly pleased with my new cook. He is trained in French and English cookery." She smiled brightly and though my audience had been rapt before, they understood their hostess's wish to move on to pleasanter subjects. They, too, began tasting and commenting and complimenting.

After their departure, my aunt, usually such a gentle

soul, rounded on me. "How could you have brought those stories of horror to my parlour?" The sound of hurt in her voice stung me.

"Forgive me, Aunt, I thought—" I looked at the satin tips of my shoes peeping out from my skirts, and thought about the workers who wove the threads and stretched the fabric, not to mention those who cleaned them when they were dirty or scuffed. "I feel so guilty for the circumstances I am in, by no virtue of my own, only luck of birth. How can I sit in such luxury every day and not attempt to help those less fortunate?"

"There is helping, and then there is upsetting my guests. Do you mean to assuage your own conscience by inflicting guilt on others?"

I did not mention that her guests appeared more fascinated than troubled. "I did not mean to do any such thing."

"You must cease this talk of prisons and reform, Lizzy. It not only hurts your marriage prospects, but if I am honest, it also makes you unpleasant company. And it helps no one."

Unpleasant company. I took that comment to heart, not because I felt overly concerned about finding a husband at present, but because if my aunt and uncle tired of me, I would be sent back to Longbourn. I bowed my head and swallowed hard. Outside, carriages rattled past, hawkers bellowed, and in every direction were exciting places to visit and sights to behold. How could I give these up?

Could I be selfish enough to turn my back on those in need for the cause of securing my own comfort? Did remaining silent on the matter for now mean I could not help in the future? No. Once I had a husband and comfortable home, I could devote my time to matters of importance such as charitable endeavours. The sad truth was that until I was settled and on my own, I was not free.

An opening door caught both of our attention, and a servant entered with a note for me.

Dearest Miss Bennet,
  I have extraordinary news! Mr Lambert and I are engaged! I wish to tell you all the details. Please call as soon as you can.
  Miss Festing

Engaged! Miss Festing had been so independent. So determined to live a life of knowledge and excitement. Would marriage change all of that? Perhaps not. Mrs Festing was the most interesting woman I knew, so perhaps marriage was not the death of intellect. In fact, it might very well be that the dull women I knew either had no natural intellect to speak of before marriage or they had been dissuaded from using it for so long that it had withered like plucked flowers. Miss Festing would be, I was certain, different, and so I would be happy for her.

I showed my aunt the note, and she clapped her hands together, likely as delighted by the news as the opportunity to escape the unpleasantness of only moments earlier. "Let us go call on her immediately!"

Typically, my aunt liked to rest after callers, but this news was, indeed, wonderful. Additionally, I believe she wanted me near the radiance of a newly arranged marriage. Unlike my mother, Aunt Gardiner was not one to speak often of marriage, but I was certain my brush with reformers had her concerned that I might grow too unconventional.

Miss Festing was aglow when we arrived, throwing her arms around me with a squeal. I was instantly caught up in her joy, allowing the day's unpleasantness and my interest in being of service to others to recede into the background. Mrs Festing and my aunt retreated to one side of the parlour, Mrs Festing's voice rising and falling in excited exhortation, though I could not discern any words.

Miss Festing and I moved across the room from them, settling onto a cream sofa with a carved gold frame, our heads bent towards one another. "Oh, Lizzy, to marry a friend! I feared I might link my life to some boor or bore, but I tell you, Mr Lambert is so perfect for me, and I hope I am equally so for him."

"I have no doubt that you are." I felt a twinge of jealousy. Would I find a man that appreciated and entertained me in the same way? I feared I would not.

Mr Darcy might have been that man, but much had changed. My chest ached at the thought of it. I would not even mention to Miss Festing that I had seen him again. This day was about her joyous news.

I asked about the date for the event and her thoughts on her gown, and that was enough to occupy us until my aunt rose, announcing it was time to depart for dinner. Miss Festing made me promise to accompany her to her appointments beginning the very next day and I agreed happily.

On the first morning, we visited the modiste. After looking at every possible available fabric in every colour, Miss Festing decided on a light pink satin silk for her wedding gown with embroidery on the front centre of the skirt and puff sleeves. Then Mrs Festing insisted they complete her trousseau with two more evening gowns, three for day, two promenade gowns, and a riding habit. So many decisions needed to be made on how to adorn them. There were laces, gatherings, collars, Spanish buttons, embroidered ribbands to go around waists, plain waists, capuchin collars, square bodices, short sleeves, longer sleeves, not to mention trimmings and tassels and clasps. By the end, we were all exhausted, and Mrs Festing's treat of delectable pastries was followed by naps at our respective homes.

On the second day, we went to the shoemaker for Miss Festing's silk slippers, and on the third, the milliner. I marvelled at the vast array of choices for her hats and bonnets, as it exceeded what I had seen at other shops, even in London. The available feathers, ribbons, and laces were seemingly endless. Sunday was for family and church, but the fourth shopping day was spent discussing food for the wedding breakfast, the fifth considering flowers, and the sixth was undergarments. Miss Festing declared she owned a broad enough array, but her mother wanted her to have a fresh start for her new life and Mrs Festing purchased every item she could think a young woman might need or desire. On the seventh day, Mrs Festing suggested we look at linen, but Miss Festing objected, saying even God rested on the seventh day. She desired a walk.

She and I strolled through the park, enjoying the view of passing carriages and children playing. Miss Festing looped her arm through mine. "How soon before I am a mother, do you suppose?"

"I should hope not until after the wedding," I teased with a grin.

She laughed. "That is only a month away! Beyond that! I wonder when, and what it shall be like."

"Being a mother?"

"And having them. And conceiving them."

I gave a giggling gasp and looked about to see who might be close enough to overhear.

"A scandalous topic, but do not fret. No one can hear us." She pulled me tighter. "I wish to know what it is like to be with a man. Mother has hinted, but never says anything specific. Do you know anything of these matters?"

"What would I know?" I shook my head. "Have you any married friends who might tell you?"

"No. They all find it too impolite to share." She frowned. "I prefer to be prepared in all things! And with no foreknowledge of the event, how am I to know how to proceed?"

It was a conundrum, and I hoped she would share with me what others chose to hide so I would not be ignorant when my time came, assuming it ever did.

"Let us hope," I said, steering her towards a pond where children were floating paper boats, "that Mr Lambert has the patience and courtesy to guide you."

"He will," she said walking ahead a bit. "He is the most patient and courteous of men!"

I was set to follow Miss Festing when someone touched my arm. I turned to see a woman in the most magnificently plumed bonnet offering a bright smile. "Miss Bennet, I am Mrs Ashburton. We met at Mrs Gardiner's home the other day."

"Of course!" We exchanged greetings and pleasantries, and then she said, "I fear your aunt was not best pleased with you the other morning."

"She did not wish me to upset her guests," I admitted. "Of course, that was not at all my intention."

"Of course not, dear. I know your aunt would keep you away from prisons and such unpleasantness, but you demonstrated such compassion and expressed a desire to be of service to those less fortunate. As it happens, I frequently visit orphan asylums. The poor dears need attention in addition to resources, and are typically such sweet things. The institutions are cleaner and safer than jails, so Mrs Gardiner might not object. I most regularly attend the London Foundling Hospital, and shall be visiting on Thursday. Would you care to accompany me? I would be glad to ask your aunt for you."

Surely my aunt could not object when it was one of her friends asking me to accompany her on her own charitable work? It was the work of a moment for me to accept. "I would love to join you."

"Wonderful." She reached into her beaded bag and brought out her card, pressing it into my hand. "Then Thursday around eleven? I will call for you in Gracechurch Street."

CHAPTER 12

The days leading up to Miss Festing's wedding were busy ones. My aunt's friend took me to a foundling hospital where I played with some of the unfortunate little ones. They were, each and all, delights, and it was difficult to pull myself away from them.

A second charitable visit to a hospital for wounded military men was not so successful. The pain and agony suffered by the poor men was heart-rending and I found I had not the stomach for the sights and sounds of it all. It compounded the guilt within me to admit it, but I reasoned that total devotion to one cause must surely be better than partial interest in many, or so I hoped.

Miss Festing's wedding day was at last upon us. My aunt, uncle, and I sat together at the church. The service was simple and brief, but lovely, and most of the women used their handkerchiefs to dab at tears as the two spoke their vows to one another.

In that moment, I thought of Mr Darcy. What would it be like to have him gaze at me the way Mr Lambert gazed at my friend, with complete love and devotion? What would it be to see Mr Darcy's smile return? To lose myself once again in his lovely green eyes? To feel my heart flutter at the touch of his fingertips on my arm?

No. No! It was imperative that I cease thinking of him in such a manner. He was lost to me the moment his brother died, and I had to look elsewhere for a match.

Returning to the Festings for the wedding breakfast, I passed through the grand entry to the ballroom. I always found the pale blue walls a soothing colour, and noted that it set off the cream plaster details of the ceiling perfectly. Yellow flowers—my friend's favourite colour—filled vases set upon the inlaid tables under each arched window. The jam tartlets were so sublime that I disregarded the rolls and meats and ate two of them. I was pleased to learn that the candied fruit and nuts in the cake were soaked in brandy rather than rum, and pondered when I would eat the piece which would be sent home with me at the end of the festivities.

Friends and acquaintances of the two families arrived in a larger number than I expected, though, given how friendly the Festings were, I ought not to have been surprised that so many desired to wish them well. Even so, there were so many in the ballroom that I waited nearly an hour to find an opportunity to speak with my friend.

"Mrs Lambert!" I said at last, kissing her cheek. "You look magnificent. The dress, the hat, the shoes. All of it has come together perfectly. And you are glowing!"

She dipped her head as if deflecting the compliment, but it was undeniable. She was radiant. At the church, she had entered looking a bit peaked and I had feared she might swoon but once Mr Lambert took her hand at the altar, her colour had returned, and her shoulders had relaxed.

On a usual day, we would have gone off together to gossip, but this was her wedding day and that would not do. Then it occurred to me that our days of scampering off to tell secrets might have ended completely. It was difficult to know how she would behave now, having entered the ranks of the married. She was my most constant companion, second only to my dear Jane of course. Would I now be alone? Lonely?

As I considered this, Mrs Festing approached and said to her daughter, "Mr Lambert is looking for you."

"In a moment." Mrs Lambert bent her head close to me once again, but her mother cleared her throat.

"Phoebe," she murmured so only the two of us could hear, "It is your duty to greet all of your guests."

Mrs Lambert blinked a few times, appearing momentarily childlike instead of a newly married woman. Her gaze dropped and she turned to leave.

"Miss Bennet," said Mrs Festing, "your gown is lovely." She kissed my cheek and smiled before departing, but it was cold comfort as I wondered in what ways my relationship with Mrs Festing also would be altered. How did unmarried friends fit into the new order?

I went to the refreshment table and saw a familiar face. "Mr Reeves!"

"Miss Bennet." His face brightened. He was as handsome as I recalled, and I felt drawn to his earnest hazel eyes and delicate jawline. His suit, however, remained unfashionably unkempt, which surprised me. I thought that for a wedding, at least, he might take some care with his appearance.

He said, "I did not think I should have the pleasure of seeing you again. I waited at St Paul's Cathedral for days, but you never returned."

"No." I glanced across the room to where my aunt was engrossed in conversation with Mrs Festing.

"Do you fear what others might think if you speak with a radical?" His lips twitched as if he was fighting back a smile.

His mocking tone irritated me. I had attended an important lecture, helped at a foundling hospital, sought out support for those in need, and made efforts to educate myself. I spoke to servants kindly and cared about others. I was hardly like many of my circle and did not care for his remarks. He scarcely knew me, after all.

I lifted my chin. "Does that amuse you?"

"In fact, it does. The provincialism that makes so many fear change and new ideas does amuse me." He lifted an eyebrow. "What exactly have I done that is so dangerous?"

I considered this. "You made me think."

Mr Reeves grasped his chest as if he had been shot. "Heavens no!" He stumbled back, nearly bumping into an older woman who glared at him, though he did not seem to notice.

I should have been filled with disdain for him, yet found him just charming enough that I did not walk away. "Are you friends with the bride and groom?"

"I am only acquainted with Lambert."

"From school?"

"And childhood. He is a family friend." His dour expression stopped my breath.

"Is he not a good man?" How could I ever be settled if my friend had married someone dishonest or unsavoury?

"He is a fine, conventional man."

"You say 'conventional' as if it were a shade in his character."

He shrugged. "It depends on the woman matched with him. Some women are suited to conventionality while others require more to be satisfied."

Did he find *me* conventional? Of course he must, for he knew nothing of the efforts I had made to learn more about and lend support to those in need. He assumed mere intentions, if that, rather than meaningful action. Although I would not tell him of my activities, I wanted him to see me more favourably.

Before I could come up with a clever retort, he added, "There is a gathering at Hyde Park tomorrow. Reformers seeking improvement to the conditions of factories. You ought to attend."

"Thank you, but I do not think my aunt will permit me to do that."

"A *conventional* stricture."

He said it casually with a little smirk, which immediately enraged me. "Do not think you understand my aunt, sir. As it happens, she and my uncle are occupied with many charities, as are their friends."

"I am sure they and their friends gladly drop their coins into the right buckets when they must," he said. "I do not censure them, I assure you. Only I had supposed you were different from them."

I felt a flush burn my cheeks. "You are incorrect in both your understanding of my aunt and her friends, and of me."

"Am I?" He shrugged. "I speak as I find."

I longed to open my lips and deliver a scathing set-down but a voice from behind me forestalled that, likely for the best. "Lizzy, you must introduce me to your friend."

"Aunt Gardiner!" My teacup rattled in its saucer as she stepped to my side. "This is Mr Reeves, the gentleman who told me of the lecture on prisons. Mr Reeves, this is my aunt, Mrs Gardiner."

My aunt's face was impassive but the twitch at her lips told me she was biting back words. Even so, she smiled and said, "Elizabeth you must come with me. I have someone I should very much like you to meet."

Knowing that denial was not a possibility, and in many ways glad for the escape from the confounding Mr Reeves, I followed her obediently. How could a man simultaneously irritate and attract me? It was different from how I felt for Mr Darcy, whose altered behaviour was due to grief, and whose new responsibilities kept him out of reach. Mr Reeves left me uncertain of whether I wanted to run towards or away from him.

"Lizzy, I cannot like that gentleman lurking about you."

"You misunderstand his intentions, Aunt, and mine. I do not have any thought for the fellow save for gratitude to him for being like-minded in our perception of society's ills."

"He is not a good influence on you," my aunt replied,

looking concerned. But for however much Mr Reeves had vexed me with his superiority and attitude, I did think he had had some good influence on me. I had no wish to be one of these ladies whose only thought was for marriage to a wealthy gentleman followed by children. Yes, I did wish for those things, but first I wished to be a part of something that really mattered.

But my aunt, worriedly frowning in Mr Reeves's direction, could never understand that and so I resolved myself not to speak of it.

CHAPTER 13

I approached Hyde Park the next day with Sarah, thinking it both exciting and foolish. I had told my aunt that I desired a walk and to look at the shops, and Sarah and I had done so. Then I suggested we enter the park, attempting to sound innocent as I claimed we were headed to Ladies' Mile. I admitted only to myself that I would quietly search the crowd for Mr Reeves, but I did not see him, which was for the best.

As we stood at the edge of the green, working men and women, even children, flooded past going towards those congregated closer to the tree line where I supposed a dais must have been erected. The protesters were wearing what appeared to be their finest—mostly inexpensive wools and cottons, but all cleaned and pressed. Many in attendance wore white, and I suspected it was to symbolise innocence or the purity of their cause. Though we were not of the same world, I felt no fear of them. They seemed passionate and earnest. I overheard bits of their chatter as they spoke to one another of better wages and working conditions, and of the drinks they hoped to enjoy after the speeches. A man tipped his hat at me, and I nodded in return, though I stole a glance at Sarah, wondering what she might think of this uninvited familiarity. She had not noticed, for she was studying the crowd, her shoulders tight. Some harder-looking men were approaching, less tidy, sleeves rolled up to their elbows, but they joined the multitudes without incident.

Though it would have been prudent to depart, I brought us to the edge of the crowd, amazed by the number of people in attendance.

Sarah seemed anxious, her voice a little tremulous as she said, "Miss Bennet, perhaps we ought to be getting back now. The Ladies' Mile is this way, and I fear a disturbance."

"Sarah, they are peaceful. Do you not see?"

Her eyes darted about and although she did not appear convinced, she remained by my side. I did not attempt to move us closer to the reformers making speeches, but on multiple occasions, the crowd near the tree line lifted their hands and fists and cheered. It was thrilling to be a part of something so large, amongst people desiring to make change and taking action. I hoped the speakers' words would be printed in the newspaper the next day so I might learn of their plans and messages.

A sound behind us caught my attention. The militia was approaching. They looked grand in their red and white uniforms, with gold epaulettes and shining buttons. Kitty and Lydia would have swooned at the spectacle, I thought, smiling.

Then I noticed the soldiers' swords were in hand, the

polished metal glinting in the sun. The faces of the militia men were hard set, and seemed almost to wish for force. That should not be. A gathering of this size might need watching lest a disturbance break out, but the crowd was peaceful. My mind was too innocent to comprehend why the soldiers would threaten violence. They began threading their way through the dense crowd before us, determination marking every step.

Another cheer sounded from the front of the crowd, then the faint strains of brass instruments reached us. Still watching the militia with consternation, I said, "Sarah, we should leave now."

Just then, I heard a scream. Beside me, Sarah gasped; as I looked at her, I heard someone else scream, this time more terribly. The crowd began running in our direction.

Couples clutching hands ran by us. Parents pulled children along quickly, their small legs moving in double time in an attempt to keep apace. A man scooped up his young son, holding him to his chest while an older child gripped onto the man's coat. A tall blonde woman shrieked as she ran past, insensible that her bonnet had fallen to the ground behind her. "Miss!" I shouted, but she did not hear me, and in any case it did not signify, for a moment later, that same bonnet was crushed by boot after boot as terrified protesters hurried out of the park as if their lives depended upon it.

Sarah tugged at my sleeve, saying, "We must hurry!" She began to push through the throng. A voice in my head said to follow her, but I stood rooted, fearful and curious at once.

The arms and swords of the soldiers were swinging

this way and that. I wanted to scream, to beg them to stop. Why were they attacking these innocent people? What crime had any of them committed? There had been no violence before their arrival. There was no reason for their blows.

An old man with blood matting his white hair limped past leaning on a cane, no doubt going as fast as he was able. The crowd was growing thicker around me, screaming, and more panicked. Realising it was past time to depart, I shook myself out of my astonished stupor. "Sarah?" I called, looking about, but I could not see her.

As I turned, someone knocked me to the ground. I hit my cheek upon falling and a boot grazed my elbow. I attempted to stand, but a girl tripped over my legs and thudded beside me, then crawled away, struggling with her skirts. I tried to push myself up again, but someone stepped on my back in their attempt to get away, then another, then another.

I suddenly realised, very acutely, the extreme danger of my situation. Would I be trampled to death? I held my arms over my head, screaming. I was frantic, certain I would be crushed in the panicked throng.

A man's hand grabbed my arm, pulled me roughly to my feet, and began to run. I stumbled to keep up. The sounds behind us were piteous and terrifying, and still we ran. A woman slammed into me, and I was separated from the man who had rescued me.

Gasping for breath, I ran across Park Lane and pressed my back against a tree. My knees trembled so I could scarcely remain upright. I stood, trying to get my breath, watching as people ran every which way, screaming and crying and bleeding.

"Miss Bennet?"

It was Mr Darcy. Seeing him, the emotions of the last minutes overwhelmed me and I began weeping with relief.

"Miss Bennet! You are crying."

"Forgive me, sir." I wiped my cheeks with my sleeve, flinching at the sting of the spot that had hit the ground.

He reached into his pocket and produced a handkerchief. "Were you caught in the melee?"

I nodded. Recalling the blood and the terror, my shoulders began to shake and, covering my face with his handkerchief, wept.

I felt fingertips on my arm for just a moment. He had reached out, but apparently realised the impropriety and pulled back. How I longed to be back in the woods of Longbourn where we could express ourselves as freely as we desired.

However, it was my duty as well to behave as expected. I took a deep breath and looked at him. His forehead was wrinkled with concern, and the expression melted my heart.

I asked, "W-were you in the park?"

He shook his head. "I had seen a gathering begin as I went to meet with my solicitor. I was leaving his offices just as the fighting broke out."

"There was no fighting. The protesters were attacked."

He cocked his head. "You were amongst them?"

What would he think if I told him the truth?

At that moment, more shouting from the park caught

our attention. "Come," he said. "My house is just this way."

I tried to follow him but when my legs almost buckled, he took my elbow and escorted me around the corner and down a street lined with beautifully appointed mansions of brick, stone and marble. In just those few steps, all was quieter and we paused a moment. "Thank you," I said, regaining myself.

"What were you doing at such a gathering?"

For a moment I considered telling him the truth: that in my determination *not* to be seen as every other gently bred young lady, I had foolishly endangered myself and gone against the wishes of my family. Instead, I said, "I was at the shops with my aunt's maid and we came upon them. I was curious when I saw so many people and wished to see what was going on." A strangled cry escaped my lips as I thought of Sarah and I added hurriedly, "I was separated from my maid. I must go back and look for her. She ran off when she saw the crowd beginning to run and I am fearful for her safety."

He held my arm tighter. "I would send out a search party, but she could be anywhere by now. She will find her way home, no doubt."

Just then a man holding a bloodied sleeve limped past and my fears for Sarah worsened.

"No," I said pulling away. "I must return and see if she is well."

"Miss Bennet," he said, standing tall so I could appreciate the fullness of his height and power, "you shall do no such thing. It is not safe, and it is my duty to return you to your aunt and uncle."

"You are more concerned with duty than what is right?"

"Performing my duty *is* what is right."

I turned the conversation. "Why are you in London? I thought you were travelling to Pemberley."

"There was a delay." His jaw was set in the same manner as when I last saw him in Meryton. The free spirit and youthful glow he had when we met two years prior were gone. He was like a dimmed lamp, and I wished I could help him.

We walked on, and, despite my recent upset, I marvelled when we entered Grosvenor Square. It was the prettiest place I had seen in London. In the middle of the square, old trees towered above an oval green surrounded by black rails. The streets were wide enough for four coaches to drive astride, and each four- and five-storey house, though different in colour and style, was perfectly ordered and balanced with columns and awnings and windows of more shapes than I knew to be possible.

We approached a gleaming white stone four-storey mansion. Its immense lacquered black doors were adorned with knockers shaped like wreaths. Mr Darcy paused at the bottom of the steps, so I assumed it was his house.

"I will have the carriage brought round to take you back to the Gardiners'. Would you like a maid to help you tidy yourself before departing?"

I looked down at my dress and brushed at the dirt. Some dust flew up and off, but some could not be removed. I regarded my hands, also covered in dirt mixed with blood from my fall. I rubbed at them but to no avail.

"I thank you, sir, but I do not wish to enter your beautiful home in such a state."

"Nonsense. I insist. You aunt will be terribly alarmed if you arrive looking thus, and my servants would be only too willing to help."

He was correct about my aunt, so I followed him up the steps and inside the grand entryway. The glorious curved staircase caught my eye first, but then I marvelled at the intricate sunburst pattern on the floor. Tall windows allowed the day's bright light to stream in, where it gleamed on the brass railing. What magnificence lay behind each closed door along the checked marble-tiled hall?

Mr Darcy spoke to a footman about readying a carriage and requested he send a maid to attend me. The footman bowed and departed. Then he stepped closer. "Let me see your hand." I held it out and he took it gingerly, frowning at the bleeding scratches on my palm. "Does it hurt?"

I shook my head; although it did hurt a moment earlier, his touch made the pain vanish.

Then his eyes met mine and my stomach flipped. As we stared at one another, the softness I remembered suffused his features, and a little smile twitched at the corners of his mouth. He reached for my face, and for a moment, I thought he might pull me into a kiss, but his fingertips grazed the bump that had formed on my cheek. He whispered, "To mar such perfection. I—"

A maid carrying a basin of water hurried into the hall and he sprang back, his hands falling to his sides.

"Miss Bennet?" the maid asked tentatively. When I

nodded, she suggested we enter a chamber where she might help me clean up.

I looked to Mr Darcy, whose face was stone once again. No, worse than stone. Pained. His desire for me pained him! Then I noticed his eyes were fixed on a portrait of his parents that hung by the foot of the stairs. His head shook ever so slightly, and he clenched his jaw. This would not do. How could I wish to be with a man who could not escape the clutches and expectations of deceased relatives?

"I shall—" I cleared my throat, hoping it might help me find my voice. "I shall merely wash my hands. There is no hope for the rest."

The maid's eyes flicked to Mr Darcy, but his gaze remained on the portrait, so she did as I requested and set the basin and cloths on a nearby table.

We finished quickly, and she curtseyed and departed. The footman approached to say the carriage was ready, and opened the door. This caught Mr Darcy's attention. His eyes drifted the length of me, catching on the still-dirty spots on my dress, but he said nothing and gestured towards the light.

My head spun as I exited the mansion, and I reached for the railing to steady myself, glad that I would be home soon.

The elegant equipage was before us and Mr Darcy was handing me in. "Thank you, sir."

Without a smile, he bowed and backed away.

As the carriage trundled on its way, I realised I still had possession of the handkerchief he had handed me. I pulled it from my sleeve and smoothed it open, noting the fine stitching in the embroidery. 'FD' was in one corner, and in the others were paisleys done in a chain stitch. I hoped it was his sister who had so lovingly decorated this cloth, and not some young lady whom he had been courting. I pressed the cloth to my face. It smelled like him: soap and cinnamon with a hint of musk. I sighed, unable to comprehend the events of the day, and sad that this might be the last bit of Mr Darcy I would encounter.

CHAPTER 14

My aunt Gardiner rushed to me in the entrance hall. "Heavens, Elizabeth! What has happened? Why were you brought home in a carriage? To whom does it belong? Is that blood? Whatever has happened to your face?"

I took her hands in mine, ignoring the sting of my palms. "I shall explain, but please may I sit first?"

She escorted me into the drawing room, and I was instantly soothed by the familiar cream walls and yellow brocade curtains, the portraits over the mantel, and her needlework left on the side table. I loved these trappings of a safe life and was relieved to be back in their midst.

Tea was poured and I attempted to hold my cup and saucer steady so as not to further worry her. I set it all down after one sip, though, then folded my hands in my lap, wanting to appear demure and obedient.

"I went shopping, as we discussed, then to Hyde Park, but there was a riot."

Her eyes flew wide. "A riot?"

How much was I to tell her? It was best to say less. "A disturbance. Sarah and I were overrun as we passed by. We were separated, and—" I clutched my hands tightly. "I do not know whether she is well. Mr Darcy found me and arranged for my delivery back to you."

"Mr Darcy? That was kind of him."

I nodded. It *had* been kind of him. He had been more like the man I had once known, yet there was still a formality and a restraint which did not allow him to be fully himself.

She called for the housekeeper, alerting her to Sarah's disappearance, and sent word to my uncle in his warehouse, though there was nothing we could do but wait and hope for her return. "Elizabeth, go bathe and ready yourself for dinner. We will send word if Sarah is located."

I stood to leave, but as I walked to the door, my aunt cried, "Are those footprints on your back?"

I recalled, then, lying on the ground feeling my breath being squeezed out with every boot sole that trod upon me. My lips quivered, but it was imperative that I not alarm her with my response so I might weep alone in my bedroom. "Aunt," I said, "I am not injured but for my scraped hands and reddened cheek." Not waiting for a reply, I hurried upstairs.

Once in my room, a servant undressed me as tears streamed down my face. I relished the warm water of the bath, though my insides roiled at the memories of the day. How could I have been so foolish? Why did I not run when Sarah suggested it? I would never forgive myself if she came to some harm. I needed to know how she fared.

The answer came within the hour. When I was back in

the drawing room, the housekeeper shared that Sarah had walked to Gracechurch Street on an ankle she had twisted as she ran from the park. I asked her to send my apologies. My aunt said I had nothing for which to apologise, but I knew that was not the truth. Perhaps my expression indicated as much, for my aunt was watchful the rest of the afternoon.

I reflected upon my actions, horrified that I had endangered this young woman as well as myself. And for what? To prove to a man I hardly knew and did not entirely respect that I was not a coward? To prove that I cared? There were other ways to prove such things. And protests were not the way to make change. Or perhaps they were, but I had not the constitution to endure another riot, and, in truth, someone such as myself, born into comfort, had no true knowledge of the injustices, and therefore, no reason to be at such a gathering. Making lives better might be my desire, but this was not how I could go about it. If I continued to worry and anger my relatives, I would lose their trust if not their favour, and would jeopardise that which I loved most: relationships, adventure, culture, and a modicum of freedom.

As much as I fancied myself independent, I was not. A man such as Mr Reeves might scoff, but in truth, I liked many of the trappings of my conventional life. Furthermore, I could be kind and generous to all, and I could treat well those in my employ when I was married and running a house of my own, but until that time, my ability to make change was limited, and my desire to rebel had been quashed.

Just before dinner, the children playing quietly at our

feet, my uncle and aunt sat reading, and I stared at the fire, a knock came at the door. Mr Reeves's card was brought in by my aunt's butler.

My aunt said, "Wood, pray tell him we are not receiving callers."

"I beg your pardon, ma'am," Wood said, "but the gentleman is quite insistent that he be granted an audience with Miss Bennet."

My aunt and uncle stared at me, though I merely returned their gaze dumbly. Why would he have come? And this was not a proper hour for calling. Had he no respect for propriety? I shook my head in wordless reply to my aunt's and uncle's stares.

In a firm voice, my uncle said, "Please tell him Miss Bennet is not receiving."

"No." I rose slowly. "I believe it would be best if I told him to leave." I kept my voice gentle so as not to alarm my aunt and uncle. "I fear he will not depart otherwise."

"Why?" My uncle's kindly face turned red.

"Please. Just give me a moment. Then I assure you, Mr Reeves will no longer be part of our lives."

They exchanged glances, and after a pause, my uncle nodded to me. I followed Wood into the hall and then the entry where Mr Reeves stood, his coat ripped, his head bandaged.

"Miss Bennet, I came to see that you had not attended the protest." I noted the blood on his collar and his knuckles. Had he fought his way out of a skirmish? Had he been trampled as I had nearly been?

"I was passing when violence erupted," I replied coolly.

"I had no idea—"

"I shall not cease in my concern for the less fortunate, but I believe this is where our friendship should end, Mr Reeves. Good day, sir."

With that, I turned and walked away, hearing Wood close the door firmly behind me.

At breakfast the next morning, my aunt said, "Lizzy, your uncle and I have hit upon the most marvellous scheme. We propose a trip to the Lakes."

I had always dreamt of visiting the Lakes, and while I suspected their main purpose was to get me away from Mr Reeves—for I imagined they did not believe me when I said I had severed all ties with the man—I was not sure that I cared. To visit the Lakes was a longstanding wish of mine, no matter how or why it came about.

CHAPTER 15

July 1811

I marvelled at how quickly arrangements could be made when one was determined, and so before I could believe my fortune, my aunt, uncle, and I had begun our journey.

It was thrilling to see the landscapes change from city to gently rolling hills to heavily wooded areas to small town and back again. Every so often, we spotted a rider or a river or a ruined castle or a grand estate or an errant sheep at the side of the road whose bleating made us laugh. The days of our journey passed pleasantly, and only once did they mention Mr Reeves, to which my cool response ended the conversation.

We reached Derbyshire and the town of Lambton, where we would spend a night. We ate a quick meal at the inn before an intended walk about the town. My aunt had often shared stories of her girlhood in Lambton, and I was interested to see the place from which she hailed, and to call upon some of her more distant relations who remained in the area.

"Lizzy, did you know that Mr Darcy's estate, Pemberley, is nearby?"

At the mention of Mr Darcy and his lands, my stomach clenched. "I had no idea, Aunt."

"I have not seen Pemberley since I was young," she continued, not noticing I was surprised by her news. "Visitors are allowed inside when the family is not about, and as luck would have it, they are away from home."

"Aunt Gardiner," I said, finding my voice, "I do not think we ought to walk about there."

"Why should we not?" she said, and I clearly heard the disappointment in her voice. "It is no different from touring Chatsworth or Blenheim and you had no objections to seeing those houses."

While I had confessed all to Mrs Lambert and Mrs Festing, I had not been as forthcoming with my aunt. And though I had told her of my feelings for Mr Darcy, I suspected she thought two and a half years since my heartbreak more than enough time to have recovered. Perhaps it ought to have been, but I had yet to cease thinking of him. Save our encounter after the riot, he had been distant—when not outright rude—the few times we had met. It was clear Mr Darcy was no longer interested in any connexion with me, not even friendship, and even if it took me another two and half years to do so, I would have to accept that.

"No one is home, Lizzy," my uncle added. "It is perfectly proper and you know it does provide a nice bit of coin for the housekeeper to lead us around. I know you are always worried for the concerns of the household."

He had me there and he knew it. A smile spread over his genial countenance as I beheld him. He was always generous in his gratuities to the servants and I would not have wished Pemberley's housekeeper to miss out on that simply because I was feeling a bit missish. If Mr Darcy and his sister were not at home, I supposed visiting Pemberley could do no harm.

I agreed without sharing my wariness. It was a challenge to force myself to climb into the carriage, and then to smile and chatter, as my aunt was wont to do, yet she was my caretaker and host on this unimaginable journey, so I did my best to hide my distress.

We entered the grounds and drove for some time through a beautiful wood. I recalled Mr Darcy explaining that the park at Pemberley was ten miles around, and that he often escaped into the surrounding woods for privacy and solace when he was young. The view was remarkable. We ascended for a full half mile and then came into a clearing where we saw, at last, Pemberley House—a large, magnificent stone building. It was beyond imagining, both in scale and beauty. If all had gone as I had once hoped it might, I might have been mistress of this place.

As we approached the door, my stomach commenced its churning. My uncle knocked—the echo of it reiterating the scale of the place—and soon the housekeeper answered the door. She was a respectable-looking older woman who introduced herself as Mrs Reynolds and explained, "The gentleman is not here at present. We expect him tomorrow with a large party of friends."

I breathed out relief that the intelligence of the innkeeper had been correct. Had we but taken one day more on our journey, we would have seen Mr Darcy, and that would not have done at all.

Mrs Reynolds first led us to the dining parlour, an enormous and yet well-proportioned room. I looked out the window as my aunt admired the table settings, which were lovely, though not as wonderful to look at as the scene outside: the river, the trees scattered on its banks, the sheep dotting the hills of the winding valley. It was so perfect it seemed more like a painting. As our tour continued through one lofty and handsome room after the next, each elegant and tastefully decorated, I could not help but continually look outside. Every window looked upon yet more beauty. To have this as one's view every day! Heavens.

As we entered a gallery of family portraits, Mrs Reynolds stopped to point out the master of the house.

My aunt said, "I have heard much of your master's fine person. It is a handsome face, but, Lizzy, you can tell us whether it is like him or not."

Mrs Reynolds' eyes widened. "Does the young lady know Mr Darcy?"

I felt my cheeks catch fire as I recalled afternoons hidden in the shadows of the trees sharing our every thought, and on the hill, lips on lips. "A little."

My aunt asked, "And do not you think him a very handsome gentleman?"

I could not force my voice out. Of course, I did. My aunt knew that that was not the problem.

Aunt Gardiner reared back, apparently realising her

misstep. My mother often made such heedless blunders, but not my aunt. Had she had too much wine at the inn before our journey?

Mrs Reynolds eyed me. "What has been your experience been with my master?

"He and his cousin, Mr Fitzwilliam, stayed a few days with us at Longbourn, my father's estate. It is in Meryton in Hertfordshire."

"Meryton?" Mrs Reynolds' voice was filled with wonder. "That is where Mr Darcy was when he received the news of Thomas... But excuse me."

She whispered something under her breath, perhaps a prayer. "Then you must be one of the Bennet family?"

I nodded, wondering how she would know of me. What had been said by him or his parents, and under what circumstances? "I am Miss Elizabeth Bennet. It was a wonderful visit," I said, "brief though it was. Mr— Colonel, now—Fitzwilliam was mildly ill, having caught a cold, which gave my family time to know Mr Darcy. Both gentlemen were kind and interesting visitors, livening up the conversation until the dreadful news arrived." I was unsure what more to say.

Mrs Reynolds' brow furrowed, and I feared I had somehow offended her, and that she would escort us out. Instead, she said, "I had never heard a cross word from Mr Darcy until his brother died, and I have known him ever since he was four years old. But these past years since his brother..." She pressed her lips together and her cheeks pinkened. "Pardon me. Shall we go on with our tour?"

She tugged at her apron and strode on. I followed hard

on her heels. "You say you have known him since he was four years old. Is that when you came to Pemberley?"

My aunt called ahead to us, "Mrs Reynolds, forgive my niece. She has a penchant for wheedling details out of everyone about their lives."

I blushed, wondering if there was some hidden rebuke in her words but my aunt seemed more amused than censuring. "I am a student of character, Mrs Reynolds, and am always eager to know where people have come from and how life has led them down their particular path."

Mrs Reynolds escorted us into the music room, where my aunt and uncle circulated to look at the fine instruments and more magnificent paintings lining the walls. As I remained at Mrs Reynolds' side, she said quietly, "I was at a neighbouring estate as the head maid when I heard the position of housekeeper was opening here at Pemberley. Everyone knew of the Darcys, of course, and Pemberley has always been known for its beauty. I never imagined I would get the position but I did and here I am, almost twenty-four years later."

"Oh, this harp!" my aunt exclaimed, peering at its pillar.

Mrs Reynolds called to her, "It is mother of pearl and onyx."

I asked, "May I enquire about what happened to the elder Darcys?"

"A tragic carriage accident on a stormy night. They ought not to have ventured out. The head coachman and one footman were also killed, and another wounded. He can no longer work, poor man. Mr Darcy still provides for the families of the deceased and the incapacitated footman, which was not required of him but certainly a vast relief to them."

She sniffed and dabbed an eye while I considered the kindness of this financial support. Mr Darcy was good at heart, despite having wounded mine.

"Let us go on with our tour." She showed us a pretty sitting room, and when I remarked that it was decorated in a style that differed from the rest of the house, Mrs Reynolds explained that it had just been redone at Miss Darcy's request.

I walked towards one of the windows, desiring to see, once again, the extraordinary view. "He is certainly a good brother."

"Whatever can give his sister any pleasure is sure to be done in a moment. She seems to be his one source of joy these days." She sighed but caught herself. "That is all of the house," she said, all business now, "that is open to general inspection. Let us return downstairs." She walked briskly and consigned us over to the gardener at the hall door.

After the door had closed and it was once again just our party, my uncle said, "What were you two speaking of, Lizzy?"

I was not sure how to answer. "The family's history."

My aunt looped her arm through her husband's. "Once she knew Lizzy and Mr Darcy were so well acquainted, her manner shifted."

I nodded. "I think she is worried about him. He has, as I said, become quite different than when I first knew him."

Uncle Gardiner asked, "Is it appropriate for a servant to share that?"

"She did not say so directly. I inferred it. She spoke of the Darcys' accident, though only briefly. I wished to know more."

"You ought not to go around asking everyone about their lives, Lizzy. You presume too much familiarity with them."

"It always seems to me that people like to talk about themselves."

"But servants?"

"Servants are people, too," I replied.

My aunt and uncle exchanged glances, and she sighed. It vexed me, and I hung back a few steps, admiring the house once again.

Suddenly, Mr Darcy appeared around the corner. It was impossible to imagine and yet there he was, standing before me. I had no way to run or hide from him, indeed nothing to do but stand there, staring, my mouth gaping inelegantly.

"M-Miss Bennet? What in heaven? Whatever are you doing here at Pemberley?"

At least I might be consoled that his astonishment appeared to match mine.

"A tour, sir," Uncle Gardiner said, stepping closer to me. "We were under the impression that you were away from home."

Mr Darcy tore his gaze from mine to look at my uncle, but returned it, making me feel like my skin was on fire. "I had been, sir. We have only just returned."

He wore the loveliest emerald velvet coat which brought out the hues of green in his dark eyes, and his hair, mussed from travel, was even more perfect. *Oh, why must I still find him handsome?*

I forced myself to speak. "I am sorry, Mr Darcy. I never would have come here if I had known you were at the house."

"No?" Hope flickered across his face, giving me pause. Perhaps he was pleased by my presence. After all, the last time we met, we had stood near one another—so near I thought he might kiss me.

"I...I was a nuisance at Grosvenor House and—"

"Not a nuisance, Miss Bennet."

We looked at one another, and perhaps he was waiting for me to say more, but all my thoughts were of whether he might ever want me to kiss him again, and of his handkerchief, which was at this moment carefully folded in my reticule.

His eye caught sight of geese flying overhead, and as he followed their path, his eyes stopped at the imposing structure of Pemberley. Instantly, his demeanour shifted. Did every reminder of his family and the expectations on him twist him so?

"You ought to be careful of ruffians and protests, Miss Bennet. I will not always be there to rescue you." His face was hard, and I could not tell if the comment was a reprimand, or guilt, or his ever-present judgment.

Rescue me? I rescued myself. Yes, he walked me away from the chaos and offered me a carriage, but I extricated myself from the violence, and surely, I could have managed to find my way home otherwise. Rescued indeed!

"May I be introduced to your friends?"

It was my cue to introduce my aunt and uncle, though

I desired nothing more than to run from this conversation. The greetings were civil, though stiff. There was a pause and then my aunt shared her admiration of the house and Mr Darcy thanked her in a gruff tone, saying it had been the work of generations and nothing within was to his taste or choice. The comment ended all future compliments my dear aunt might have shared.

Two geese from the pond down the hill squawked their fury at one another. If only we humans were as free to share our true opinions.

My uncle said, "We ought to be leaving."

Mr Darcy looked as if he might say something, but when he did not, I bade him farewell and curtseyed, my stomach roiling.

Another figure rounded the corner, "Fitzwilliam, why do we not have our tea out— Oh!" A pretty blonde girl of fifteen or sixteen stepped to Mr Darcy's side. From the likeness to her portrait, I realised it was Miss Georgiana Darcy. This was confirmed when her brother introduced us.

"Miss Bennet?" she said. "At our home? Why, I have heard ever so much about you!" She stepped towards me and took my hands, pressing them, and who was more astonished, Mr Darcy or I, would be impossible to say. "Will you stay for tea?"

Mr Darcy and I both said, "No," simultaneously, though I added a softer "thank you" as well.

Miss Darcy stared at her brother, her brow furrowed, but before she could ask more, I said, "My aunt and uncle and I have plans to see more sights before it grows dark, but I thank you for your invitation, Miss Darcy."

Her name came from my lips more pointedly than I had desired. "I do hope we shall be better acquainted one day. I hear you are an accomplished musician and draw beautifully. Perhaps in the future you might prove how right your brother was when he shared his praises of you."

She immediately demurred, her countenance gaining two bright red spots that I deduced had nothing to do with the heat. She is shy, I recognised, and doing all she can to exert herself on my behalf.

"Perhaps you could come tomorrow then?" she asked hopefully.

What was the meaning of this interest she had in me? Had Mr Darcy confessed to his younger sister—his ward and one much his junior—the nature of our now-ancient and very brief relationship? It seemed unlikely. Or was it?

Mr Darcy was staring at the ground, his jaw tight and his fists clenched by his side.

I would rescue him, though he did not deserve it. "We must depart the region in the morning, so I fear that I cannot accept. But I thank you for your kindness."

To this, Mr Darcy merely bowed and walked away. His sister offered a hurried curtsey and followed him.

"I do not understand," Miss Darcy said as they disappeared around the corner, and I heard nothing more.

My aunt, uncle, and I walked to the carriage in silence, leaving me in a swirl of terrible thoughts. Mr Darcy must have thought that I had purposely thrown myself in his way, and there was no way to assure him that I had not. Had we only departed ten minutes sooner or had he and his sister not returned early, this entire debacle might have been avoided.

I blushed at the thought of him again, and cursed myself for my feminine weakness, as well as my poor choice of parting words. And yet he was rude. It was clear he wanted no part of me in his life. Or did he? There had been moments when an attraction was apparent, but it would vanish as quickly as it surfaced. Could I desire a man so unpredictable? No. Upon reflection, it *was* predictable. Whenever he was reminded of his position and duty, he retreated into an emotional prison. Was it a prison of his own making or one he was required to live in unhappily? Either way, it was one in which I was not welcome. I could only hope that the future would bring no more of Mr Darcy.

No, I did hope for him. Why could I not stop?

CHAPTER 16

August 1811, Ramsgate

The water glimmered to the horizon, and boats dotted the blue sea here and there. I breathed a huge sigh of satisfaction at the glorious sight. "Mary, is it not magnificent?"

My sister smiled, but it was weak. I put an arm around her and led her a few steps along the sea wall. "Are you cold?"

"Not at all, Lizzy. The day is warm."

"Yes, but you take a chill easily." Although I was in a thin muslin dress, she was wrapped in two thick shawls and I still could feel her shiver. At least she had worn a cornette so her head would be warmer. She had been wasting away to the point that, when I arrived at Longbourn to collect her, I had gasped. Her cheekbones were pronounced, and her shoulder blades poked out when I hugged her. My hope was to keep her well for our adventure without dwelling upon the inevitable: my sister would not survive the year. No, that was optimistic. Mary likely would not live to see the leaves change colour in autumn. We had been told she had a cancer, an illness we did not understand even if we had long known it would eventually cause her death. It was a strange disease, marked by bouts of relative good health and rapid descents into illness; we always held out hope that the good times would eventually prevail. Alas, as she had weakened, those hopes had dimmed. We had come to Ramsgate in hopes of restoring her vigour though I feared it would be a last holiday instead.

I held tightly to her arm as we walked. "Tell me when you need to return to our lodgings."

"I desire," she breathed heavily, "to sit on that bench, not to return. I hope to—" There was a pause as she gathered herself. "I hope to be out as much as possible. To waste what time I have in a gloomy room is unthinkable."

To consider her *demise* was unthinkable—at least to me. Mary was facing it all, at least outwardly, with impressive and astonishing bravery.

Oddly, her illness had brought us closer together. Since receiving Jane's letter while in the Lakes telling me Mary had taken a turn and was once again suffering the effects of her disease, I had taken on her care, never regretting for a moment that my journey with the Gardiners had been cut short. My aunt and uncle had brought me back quickly to Longbourn and returned to London after only a day's visit, promising to return my belongings, which I had left at Gracechurch Street. Perhaps they ran off because, as they said, it was too crowded at Longbourn, but they had stayed at length with their children in prior years. I suspected the unpleasantness of Mary's death sentence was what sent them off. My mother was nearly mad in her distress over my sister's illness and as much as my aunt loved her sister-in-law, Mama could scarcely speak without weeping, which Mary declared disconcerting and begged her to stop.

Watching Mary and Mama's interactions, I had decided the situation would not do, and asked Mary whether she would like to travel. Curled up on an overstuffed chair in her room, having just recovered from another incidence of unexplained fever, she had sat up, her face brightening. "I have always longed to see the sea. Would you—could you arrange it?"

I promised that I would.

I suggested my parents join us on this sojourn, but neither would agree, and Jane declined, as well. Were they afraid? Did they not care enough? Were they exhausted from having nursed her to this point? No one would say, but I was thrilled by the idea of another adventure.

Mary and I were sent to Ramsgate with our maid Bridget, who was likely not quite old enough to be a true companion to us but would do well enough to avoid gossip or suspicion. We were told that our aunt and uncle Philips would arrive the following week. They would not have been the relations I would have chosen for a holiday but it seemed to satisfy everyone else. After the three-week stay, we would return home—if Mary was well enough to travel. I had to believe she would be.

"Our rooms are not gloomy," I said, thinking that the bright sitting room with a window facing the sea was lovelier than I could have hoped for.

She closed her eyes and lifted her face to the sun in a manner that reminded me of a sunflower. A pale one. "I prefer being outdoors."

I laughed. "When we were young, you hated fresh air."

"The air was fine." She leant against me and I relished the weight of her. "It was the bugs I loathed."

"And the dirt."

"And the snakes."

"Snakes?" I leant away to see her face. "I never once saw a snake in all my walks."

Mary smiled and opened her eyes. "I always imagined there were snakes in every hedge." She shrugged. "You seemed to enjoy your privacy anyhow, Lizzy. I never wished to interrupt."

Was that true? I recalled loneliness and pleasure in equal measure. Had I created my own solitude and the distance between myself and this sister? I had been impatient with her tendency towards pedantry and judgmental of her interests. I still was, as a rule, though it all had changed the moment I knew I would lose her. What a terrible shade in my character; what a waste of hours we could have spent not only as sisters but as friends. But if I could not atone for my past sins, I would at least savour the last moments we had as best I could.

I took her hand. "I cannot account for my behaviour in the past, Mary. I can only say from this moment forward, I shall be at your service indoors and out. Should you like to bathe in the sea? I could hire a bathing machine. Papa has been shockingly liberal in providing me funds for this holiday."

She shook her head. "I am afraid I am too weak. What if I were swept away?"

I laughed. "Then the bathing machine would keep you in, or I would hold you. If sea bathing is not something of interest, we could attend a concert or a lecture. Of course, we could also simply sit and have tea." I looked at the boats. Some were making progress across the expanse of sea while others idled. "Who do you think is out there?"

"They do not look like fishermen. Pleasure-seekers, I suppose."

"Well, yes, but *who* are they? Do you not wish to know? They could be a family enjoying the sea air, or a soldier having rented a boat to say goodbye to his sweetheart while a chaperon looks on, or illicit lovers with no chaperon at all and no one to stop them."

"Lizzy!" She looked at me askance, and we laughed. "Perhaps you are in need of more serious reading to quiet your wild imagination."

"You have tried for years to persuade me to read more serious things. I do not possess your patience for philosophy and sermons."

"You do not have patience for much of anything that interests me. Few do." She tried to stand but needed help, so I took her by the elbow. "My own patience was misguided, however. I do not have time left to wait for love, or a family, or any of that."

There was a melancholy in her voice and I determined to amuse her the rest of the afternoon. At Mary's wish, we began to walk towards the hotel, with Bridget following a few paces behind. "Lizzy, promise me you will not wait for the perfect man. He does not exist. You must marry so you may have security and children, for you would be so good with little ones."

"I fear I would not. I am nothing like Jane, who will make a perfect mother one day."

"Yes, Jane is exceptionally patient with children, but as you can see from who is here with me and who is not, you are a caretaker at heart. I am in earnest. Marry a decent man. He need not be the most handsome, the most exciting, or have the greatest fortune. He simply needs to suit you well enough."

I chose not to argue that I hoped for more than simply 'decent' and 'well enough'. Perhaps she was correct, but it seemed too soon to settle. For her, it was already too late. Oh Mary!

We strolled on, slowing occasionally for her to regather her strength, and at last reached the hotel. As we crossed the expansive lobby, Mary eased away from me saying she would be too weary for dinner or even tea. "Let Bridget escort me upstairs. Enjoy the remains of the day."

They walked to the stairs, leaving me to wonder how I would spend my time when I was unaccompanied. I did not wish to remain in our apartment, but until my aunt and uncle Philips arrived, it would be improper for me to do much else.

At that moment, I heard my name and turned my head, astonished to see Miss Darcy waving at me, an older woman standing at her side. When I approached, she beamed, introducing me to Mrs Younge, her companion. Miss Darcy said they had arrived in Ramsgate only hours earlier and expressed her pleasure in seeing me again. "We were just off to take tea. Would you care to join us?"

"Will your brother be there?" The thought of sitting at a table with him filled me with dread.

She shook her head, so I agreed. As we began to walk, she looped her arm through the crook of my elbow and began to chatter. What a trusting and friendly young woman!

We entered the tea room and were seated, and even after we ordered, Mrs Younge sat passively watching us. I thought to engage Mrs Younge in the conversation, but Miss Darcy had a great deal to say, making me reconsider my prior determination of her as shy. Indeed, it seemed she needed very little prompting. "Tell me of your music. What do you enjoy playing most?"

She described her preferences in both playing and listening, and shared that while in London, she had the great pleasure of attending numerous concerts in private homes and at the Opera House. She even enjoyed the musicians who played on the streets and in the parks all over London. "Being in town is such an improvement over my lonely existence in Derbyshire."

"Had you no friends near Pemberley?"

"Not very close, no. At school in town, I formed attachments, but some of the older girls have already married, and others have returned home to prepare for the upcoming Season. My brother has at last allowed me to leave school and since then, Mrs Younge has been my most constant companion."

Again, this would have been the time to ask Mrs Younge about herself, but just as I began to form a question, a plate of sweets arrived. Miss Darcy delighted in them.

"We have a very fine bake shop in Meryton and I did not expect to find its equal in Ramsgate."

"My brother recently mentioned eating marzipan there. What a funny thing to remember, for that must have been several years ago now."

Why would that have stood out? At first, I was not certain, but then remembered that that outing had ended with the most remarkable conversation and near-kisses under a canopy of trees. I lowered my face to hide the blush that threatened to betray my thoughts.

I had turned to Mrs Younge to ask if she would desire something more savoury when a gentleman stopped at our table.

"George!" Miss Darcy said, clapping.

Mrs Younge looked up, her face blank. "What a surprise to find you here, Mr Wickham."

CHAPTER 17

The handsome gentleman was all smiles as he bowed and said, "Georgiana! I had no idea you would be in Ramsgate."

"A marvellous coincidence! Miss Bennet, may I introduce you to Mr George Wickham. George, this is my companion, Mrs Younge, and my new friend, Miss Elizabeth Bennet. She is an acquaintance of my brother."

A darkness flickered across his face when she said the word 'brother', but he covered it smoothly and bowed again. "I do not wish to intrude on your tea."

"Not at all!" Miss Darcy said. "Do not leave. There is another chair and plenty of food."

He looked to me and I nodded, so he sat. Mrs Younge continued to sit quietly sipping and nibbling as the rest of us became better acquainted. Mr Wickham was charming and handsome—a rare combination, as many handsome men relied on their looks to make themselves passable company, and many men were entertaining while their looks were nothing to speak of. And charm was even more rare than entertaining.

Mr Wickham asked whether my visit to Ramsgate had been pleasant thus far. I did not wish to burden him with the details of the sad reason for my journey to this seaside town, and simply agreed that yes, Ramsgate was, indeed, pleasant.

He and Miss Darcy laughed and shared stories of her youth, telling a particularly amusing tale of her hiding under the pianoforte when one set of guests were about and refusing to emerge, even when the group had moved rooms. Mr Wickham said, "In the end, Thomas and I flushed her out like a cat, one approaching from behind to scare her out of the spot and the other in front receiving her with love."

"Which were you?" I asked.

"The love," she announced, turning pink with pleasure at the memory. "Thomas was always rather stern." Her smile faded. "I ought not to speak ill of him. Forgive me. May he rest in peace," she added under her breath.

"No apologies are necessary. He was as you say, a stern and serious man. It did not make him a bad person, but severity was part of his character." She nodded and he touched her cheek. At her behest, he shared tales of his recent travels about England, and even when the topics were common, such as hiring a horse or locating lodgings, the skill of the speaker was such that it rendered the subject interesting.

I asked, "How long have you been venturing about?"

Mr Wickham straightened. "Since the death of Lady Anne and Mr Darcy." Miss Darcy looked down and he took hold of her hand with brotherly affection, leaning in and whispering something in her ear that brought the smallest of smiles to her lips.

Miss Darcy said to me, "Mr Wickham grew up at Pemberley. He is like family to us all, my father most particularly."

A heavy silence hung between us.

"And what do you do with your time, Mr Wickham?" I asked. "Have you some career or is that not a necessity?"

His eyebrows lifted. "A complicated question, and one best left for another time." He folded his napkin and rose, explaining that he had an appointment but appreciated our allowing him to sit with us. Despite Miss Darcy's protests, he departed, assuring her he would see her again soon.

Little did we know this surprise reunion was all part of a plan.

The next morning, Mary and I walked down the pier—eight hundred feet out to sea! It was a feat of engineering that left us both aghast. For a moment, I faltered and said we might plummet into the water, but Mary's rational mind won the day by reminding me that I go into buildings and cross bridges that require skill to design and construct every day, so this should be no different. My younger sister took hold of my arm and promised to protect me should the entire structure crash down. It was laughable all around, but it further brightened the sunny day.

There were more soldiers about on land and a few military boats in the harbour. Some sort of deployment must have been occurring, but no one we asked seemed to know exactly who was called or to where they might be travelling. Nothing more than 'the war' was offered by way of explanation. The remarkable thing was how little a war just across the sea could change our lives, and I felt a pang of guilt at the ease of my life when death was so near.

Mary stumbled, reminding me that death was even nearer than I cared to admit, but I merely smiled and carried on as if all was well.

We watched seagulls swarming near an older couple who were flinging bits of bread into the air, and we laughed when a passing woman screamed as one bird swooped so close to her face that her bonnet nearly flew off in the wake of it.

Mary was more energetic than she had been of late, so after the pier, we ventured to the library, a spacious and elegant building with views of the French coast and the Downs. Mary and I each borrowed books, as did Bridget, and we walked back to the hotel.

I said to her, "I wish to have a dress made for you."

"What a waste! Even if I live another ten years, you know I have no interest in fashion."

"Mary, it might be nice to have something pretty to wear. Let us at least look."

Her initial expression was of full disapproval, but she eventually softened to potential acquiescence.

As we approached the hotel, I noticed Mr Wickham sitting out front. We greeted each other and I introduced my sister. When he suggested a walk, I explained we had just returned from one, but Mary told him I never tired and urged me to go. "Lizzy, if you would like to venture out again, I shall not mind. Bridget may accompany you and we shall reconvene for dinner. I am in need of rest, but do not wish to miss another meal, for your descriptions make me envious of the restaurant's offerings."

After bringing Mary to our room and ensuring her comfort, Bridget and I returned to Mr Wickham. "I thought you might be with Miss Darcy."

He smiled. "She and Mrs Younge are looking at hat trimmings, so I left them."

"Hat trimmings do not delight you?"

"My own hats are trimmed well enough, thank you." He laughed. "And I do not enjoy shopping half so much as engaging in a stimulating conversation with a handsome woman."

I felt my cheeks warm and began to walk. "You are a skilled flatterer."

"So I have been told. Lady Anne was particularly fond of my efforts."

"I am perplexed, Mr Wickham, at never having heard of you from Mr Darcy. I did not know him for long, but another person in the house, and one as close as you seemed to be to the family, would have deserved mention. Or so I should have thought."

His jaw set, and I regretted my enquiry immediately, but before I could apologise for my indelicacy, he said, "I am glad you asked." His frown betrayed his word choice, but I felt assured that he would not abandon our walk and refuse to speak to me in the future. "I can tell you much of the Darcys, as I have been connected with them since infancy."

A vendor was selling small bags of nuts, and though I declined, Mr Wickham bought some for himself and held the bag out. I took one to be polite, enjoying its sweet roasted crunch more than expected. The next vendor had cherries on sticks, but both of us feared dripping juice on our clothes and passed with some regret, for the fruit was tempting.

"How were you connected to the family?"

"We grew up together in the same house. We were educated together and played together, for my father worked for Mr Darcy as his steward. The elder Mr Darcy often acknowledged himself to be under the greatest obligation to my father's active superintendence of Pemberley property. Before my father's death, Mr Darcy promised to provide for me. But the younger Mr Darcy did not keep this promise."

"How abominable!" We walked a few steps before I worked up the courage to ask, "Has Mr Darcy changed so completely? Has he lost all feeling? I knew one man before the death of his brother and parents and met an entirely different man in recent years. It is unnerving to see the change, if I am honest."

"You could not have met a person more capable of giving you certain information on that head than myself. Has Mr Darcy changed? Perhaps. He always had traces of cruelty within him, but his dispassion and lack of care have deepened since the loss of his family."

Cruelty? I could not align that word with the Mr Darcy I knew, but I did not say as much.

"The world is blinded by Mr Darcy's fortune and consequence, or frightened by his high and imposing manners, and sees him only as he chooses to be seen."

Even after his cold welcome when last we met at Pemberley, such a description did not match the man I had first known. From what I heard of Mr *Thomas* Darcy and of the elder Darcys, certainly. But Mr Fitzwilliam Darcy?

"His father was one of the best men that ever breathed, and the truest friend I ever had. I can never be in company with Fitzwilliam Darcy without being grieved to the soul by a thousand tender recollections of his father, the better man."

Mr Wickham crumpled the now-empty bag and shoved it in his pocket. "The late Mr Darcy was my godfather and meant to provide for me amply. He thought he had done it, but when the valuable living in Kympton that he meant for me became available, it was given elsewhere."

"You wished to take orders?" Somehow Mr Wickham's demeanour did not give him out to be a man of God. In London, Mr Reeves had commented on the selfish reasons men he knew at university went into the ministry. We had even joked that it was only to gain more sipping chocolate. Was Mr Wickham such a man, consumed more by earthly comforts than being of assistance to others? I knew too well how few professional opportunities were left to men of certain breeding, but Mr Wickham was not the second son of a great man, so he could have entered areas of trade with no disgrace.

"I was brought up for the church, and I should, by this time, have been in possession of a most valuable living, had it pleased our mutual friend."

Nausea rose as I thought of Mr Darcy's unkind words at the assembly, and our strained interaction at Pemberley. "I am not sure either of us dare call him a friend. What shall you do now?"

He paused and leant against a stone wall overlooking the sea. "A military life is not what I was intended for, but now I strive for a commission. However, as the late Mr Darcy's wishes have been ignored, I have no means to purchase one."

"I cannot understand how the late Mr Darcy's will could be disregarded. Have you no legal redress?"

The wind blew his light brown hair, styled into tamed wildness by a pomade that smelled of citrus. It made him doubly attractive, but his grim expression refocused my thoughts.

"There was an informality in the terms of the bequest as to give me no hope from the law. No man of honour could have doubted the intention, but Darcy chose to doubt his father's intentions—or treat it as a merely conditional recommendation and assert that I had forfeited all claim to it by extravagance."

Dare I ask? I could not help myself. "What sort of extravagance?"

He turned to face me. "I admit I have not always behaved in a fashion I am proud of. I indulged in youthful indiscretions and had a certain carelessness with funds. I am since reformed. Truly." Perhaps my face displayed scepticism or disapproval, for he added, "I have a warm, unguarded temper, and I may have spoken too freely with Mr Darcy in the past, but I am not as he sees me. The fact is, we are very different men. He hates me."

"Hates you? That is a strong assertion."

"Strong, yet true." He began to walk again. "It is a dislike which I cannot help but attribute in some measure to jealousy. Had the late Mr Darcy liked me less, his younger son might have borne me better."

"Did you get on with Thomas Darcy?"

"Certainly. Even though he was older, I was more a brother to him than was Fitzwilliam. So you see, it was inevitable that, being left with all of the riches and power, he would wield both to punish me for the preferences of his deceased father and elder brother."

All the while we were talking, clouds had gathered on the horizon and were approaching.

He seemed to notice, as well. "I think it best we get back inside before the rain arrives."

CHAPTER 18

That evening, Mary and I went to the dining room and enjoyed a wonderful dinner together. Given her frequent complains of stomach distress and winces of pain that left her clutching her swollen belly, I was relieved to see her consume much of the meal. She relished each bite, especially the sweets—a category of food she had dismissed in her younger years as an unnecessary indulgence.

"Do you think we could get Cook to learn to make ice cream?" Mary asked, her eyes closed as she savoured the last bite.

"I dare you to ask!" We both laughed heartily, for Cook hated any and all requests, and the idea of her using any of her precious ice for a treat was impossible to imagine. "Perhaps she could learn to make meringue to go around a cake?"

"I dare *you* to ask."

"You must do it. She would not refuse someone—" I pressed my lips together, cursing my loose tongue.

"Someone who is dying?" she asked with only a small falter. It was like being stabbed in the heart, but her smile brightened. "It would be worth attempting, for I should so like more meringue." She set her hand on mine and squeezed. "Lizzy, we must be able to speak of it honestly."

"Yet I need not joke about it." I pulled my hand back. "You were right in your criticisms of me. I am too merry and often at inappropriate times."

"Too merry? If only I could be accused of such a thing. My last days shall be spent in lightness when possible. Do not fret." She looked about for a waiter. "I desire more cake."

"Mary, you will burst!"

"What a better way to die than slowly and not eating." She waved at the waiter. "Shall we share or will you want your own?"

After Mary ordered one more piece of cake, I suggested that we go out on the morrow for a walk and shop for a new gown and what Miss Darcy referred to as 'magnificent fripperies'. Mary agreed reluctantly, and the following morning, as we approached the dressmaker's shop, I had high hopes. How different this was from shopping with Mrs Lambert, whose latest letter had arrived at the hotel just the day prior. It was filled with joyful tales of her honeymoon and new house, which she said I must visit in town soon and help to decorate. While I had no talent for design, I thrilled at the idea of seeing my dear friend again, though when that might be, I could not say. I had been so little at Longbourn in the past two years, I knew not how long my father would tolerate it, or continue to fund me.

At the door, I said to Mary, "We need only look at

designs. If you honestly do not want any of what the modiste has to offer, we shall leave."

As soon as we entered, we were greeted by an assistant who introduced herself as Miss Blair, a young woman with an open smile and sparkling blue eyes. I told her that Mary was looking for a dress without much fuss, and one that would not take a very long time to finish—the words caught in my throat but likely sounded like an item merely sought by an impatient customer.

"Allow me to show you what I have that is already almost ready," Miss Blair offered.

While this excited me, Mary's reserve continued. "My willingness shall depend on the style."

"Of course," Miss Blair said, with a reverent bow of the head. "I feel confident we can find you something. We have designs that are appropriate for the seaside, but that can be worn in other locales as well."

She brought Mary to a bright corner of the shop and held up a gown with a full neck ruff and a striped pelisse. As much as Mary preferred modesty, the ruff, I knew, would be too much adornment, and was roundly rejected. Miss Blair showed us a morning dress in evening primrose sarsenet; Mary shook her head so the girl retrieved a walking dress. It was a muslin robe, which seemed promising until we spotted the square neckerchief folds. Even I thought it was too fancy.

Finally, we were shown a simple muslin with long sleeves and a plain collar. Mary approved but was concerned about being chilled. I assured her we could secure a new shawl to match, if she so desired, but she said she would use ones she already owned. I chose not to press her on the matter. Economy would always be the thing that pleased her most.

Miss Blair called for a seamstress who would fit Mary's dress, then said to me, "And for you, Miss?"

"I have as many gowns as I desire at present, but I thank you."

Disappointment flicked across the shopgirl's face, but she curtseyed and left us to the fitting.

"You may have this one altered for you eventually, Lizzy."

I sighed. "Mary, please do not say such things."

"Even if they are true?"

"Many things are true, but we do not speak of them."

Mary pressed her lips together and continued with the fitting in silence. I feared the outing was ruined, but when the seamstress told her to take one last look in the mirror, Mary smiled, making a quarter turn one way then the other, then gave a full spin.

"My, my, Sister. One would almost think you noticed how pretty you are."

She cocked her head. "Vanity is a sin. But I suppose admiring God's creation at times cannot be entirely wrong."

I clapped. "Well said!"

As she took one more look in the mirror, I noticed a new bruise on the back of her thin wrist. I bit my lip, despairing at each bit of evidence that my sister was slipping away.

When all was settled, we returned to the hotel. Mary wanted to read quietly for a time, so I went to call on Miss

Darcy in her rooms, as she had suggested we might take a walk today.

I approached her door and knocked, but no one answered. A chambermaid passed me in the hall, and said, "Beg your pardon, Miss, but the lady is out. She left not a quarter of an hour ago." As I thanked her, the young woman's bucket slipped from her hand and I reached for it, slopping water on my hem and slippers.

She yelped, and began a profusion of apologies, but I assured her, saying, "It is remarkable how clean I have kept since coming to Ramsgate. Typically, I am in disarray daily! I have no new ways to apologise to our maids, but they are gracious."

As she still looked stricken, I said, "You must have a record of good work to offset this incident if anyone found out. And I shall not mention it to a soul, I promise you."

Her shoulder relaxed. "I do very good work, Miss. Always have."

"How long have you been here?"

She looked to each end of the hall as if ensuring none were about to see her speaking to a guest. Her voice low, she said, "Two years. And six before at a house in Margate."

"You are so young. How old could you have been when you began work?"

"I have always worked, Miss. It is a relief and pleasure to work for pay. I was eight when I left home and became a scullery maid."

"So young! How did you manage to carry heavy pots at such a young age?" I knew not how old she might be now, but she was even more petite than I. At age eight, her buckets must have been larger than she was.

She laughed, and I marvelled at her humour over her challenging past. "Once I pitched headfirst into the pot used for porridge. It was so large Cook had to help me get out! The kitchen was dull, but here there is always something entertaining—though I ought not to say." She bobbed a curtsey and lifted the pail.

I reached into my reticule. "My name is Miss Bennet. I am in apartment three. If you see Miss Darcy return, would you tell her I should be pleased to have her call on me in my rooms?" When I pressed the coin into her hand, she beamed and assured me she would.

An hour later, a knock on the door alerted me to the chambermaid's presence. "Miss Darcy has returned and asked me to send a message that she and Mr Wickham are taking tea together and would be pleased to have you join them. Your sister, as well, if she so desires."

I thanked her kindly, and Mary and I readied ourselves to go downstairs. The tea was a pleasant diversion and enjoyed by all. As before, Mr Wickham had no shortage of entertaining stories and kept us laughing for nearly two hours. As we rose and walked out of the tea room, Mr Wickham asked whether I would be attending the ball at the hotel the next evening.

I pondered his question. I had not intended to do so but was finding the pattern of my evenings—a short walk with Mary followed by reading until sleep—too repetitive.

"Yes, I would enjoy it very much." He smiled and I was glad, though decided to add a caveat. Seeing that Mary and Miss Darcy were far enough ahead that I could not be overheard, I said, "I will require, sir, that—should she be well enough for exertion—you dance with my sister Mary."

Before he could react—for I could not bear any negative comment or expression—I said, "Your kindness to my sister will be appreciated."

He put a hand over his heart and bowed his head. "It would be my pleasure, I assure you."

CHAPTER 19

The next afternoon, Aunt and Uncle Philips arrived with their predictable noise and fanfare. They had many trunks and servants, and their voices were loud as they directed the footmen where to put their belongings. In all of the commotion, they did not realise that Mary and I stood awaiting their notice.

"Mary! Lizzy!" my aunt said at last. "These servants are fools. It should be obvious where things go and yet they know nothing." I cringed but she continued. "Not a brain between 'em. Money seems not to buy good help."

I attempted to catch the eye of a servant hanging a coat in the armoire, but he averted his gaze immediately.

"In London, so many are starving. One would think there would be eager men about with some care for their work." She turned in a circle. "These rooms will do. For what we paid, they should, but one never knows whether a place will disappoint." She walked to the window, touched the heavy striped curtain and nodded with approval. "Quite a view, if it were not raining. How has the weather been?"

Mary said, "Glorious, really. Each day has felt like a gift."

Her words reminded me of the invitation to the ball. "Oh Mary, I nearly forgot. What say you to attending the ball tonight?"

She appeared a little dubious, though surprisingly tempted. "We are not subscribers. It is twice the price."

"Would you want to subscribe and attend week after week?" When Mary smirked, I said, "So the price is not the issue. And before you argue that we have nothing to wear, rest assured that Mama had our gowns and slippers packed."

"You must!" exclaimed Aunt Philips. "What better place to find a husband, Lizzy. And Mary, it would do you good to exert yourself."

My aunt knew nothing of what would do Mary any good, and the comment about husbands stung Mary, and me on her behalf. Nevertheless, a ball would be enjoyable, and Mary was having a good day, having eaten a decent breakfast and walked to and from the dining room without complaint.

Aunt Philips added, "I love nothing more than a ball!" and we knew there was no refusing her.

That evening, we entered the ballroom accompanied by our aunt and uncle, as well as Mrs Younge and Miss Darcy.

Mr Wickham was already inside and swept in for greetings. "Ladies, who would prefer which dance, for I intend to dance with each of you. If that is agreeable to you, of course."

"Everything is agreeable when it is with you, George!" Miss Darcy curtseyed to match his bow.

"Mary," I said, "would you prefer a Scotch reel, a country dance, or a cotillion?"

"A country dance. My understanding is that they play them slower here, so I might manage the entire time."

Mr Wickham held out his elbow, explaining which was next, and they ventured to the bottom of the line. I was pleased to see Mary engaging in conversation and acknowledging those around her. Had our home been what held her back? Was it too stultifying? Too rigid? Too predictable, each of us having our expected role? Or was her impending end giving her permission to go beyond the confines of her past? This thought did not make me overly sad, for I was witnessing her happiness on the arm of a handsome man who appeared to be enjoying her company.

"He is a kind soul," said Miss Darcy of Mr Wickham, "and speaks easily with most. Everyone but my brother, I fear."

Her mention of Mr Darcy was like a slap. I cleared my throat. "Was it always thus?"

"For as long as I can recall. I know not why."

My aunt said, "We shall dance, shall we not, Mr Philips?" He took her elbow, and as they began towards the dance floor, she called over her shoulder, "Find a husband, Lizzy! Or at least a dance partner."

I winced and caught Miss Darcy's eye.

She looked at me with some pity, and was kind enough to change the subject. "Shall we find refreshments?" We walked with Mrs Younge to the tables laid out with food and drinks, and each of us selected a cup.

"I have had a letter from my brother. He says he shall arrive within the week for a visit."

Mrs Younge choked, and her teacup rattled on its saucer.

"Are you all right?" Miss Darcy asked, and Mrs Younge nodded, dabbing at her lips with her napkin.

"How long shall Mr Darcy stay?" I asked, feeling the familiar mix of longing and disappointment.

"I do not know. He is unpredictable. I am surprised he is even coming. He prefers the woods to the sea."

The woods. Yes, secluded, secretive, quiet. Romantic.

We spoke of places she had visited with her brother as well as the rest of her family. She said the Lakes were her favourite destination. I had loved my time there before the letter about Mary arrived, and shared as much, adding that I longed to travel more, though not to the Lakes, as that place was somewhat tainted for me now. Perhaps, I thought, I would find a husband with the resources and desire to see the world. Mr Darcy had wanted that. *Mr Darcy.* I sighed. Alas Mr Darcy had wanted that, but not me along with it.

Mary and Mr Wickham joined us before the dance was at its end, for she had grown too exhausted to continue. Even so, both were laughing and desperate for something to drink. It was wonderful to see Mary happy. I did not think she imagined herself in love with Mr Wickham, but I supposed it was exciting for her to have a man's attention that did not feel like pity.

When the next song was set to begin, Mr Wickham held out his elbow. "Come, Miss Bennet. It is our turn." As we walked to the dance floor, he remarked on Mary's surprising agility.

"Surprising in what way?" I feared that in appearing so severe in the way she wore her hair and the dull colour of most of her gowns, she gave the impression that she could not enjoy herself. But that was not what he said. It was agility.

"For a time, she moved as well as any healthy woman."

"She has been filled with energy today. It is uncertain how long it will last, but I take each day as a gift."

"You are a gift to *her*. And what a place to stay! I am told by Miss Darcy that your apartment looks directly towards the sea."

The couples readied themselves to begin and we checked our positions. "My aunt and uncle are very generous to situate us here. My family could not be so extravagant."

He cocked his head. "Do you not live on a grand estate?"

"Grand?" I laughed. "Indeed not, sir. We have lands that have been in our family for generations, but—" It occurred to me that sharing my family's challenges with money was not appropriate. "My father's estate is entailed and when he dies, we shall become what is known as the genteel poor—unless we marry men of great fortune, which is not likely."

The musical introduction began and we were off. While it was pleasurable to move swiftly and on the arm of a man so pleasing to look at as Mr Wickham, I could not help but note a trace of trepidation that I had not seen when he was with Mary. What could be troubling him? Perhaps he did not know these steps as well? I thought not. Could it be that he thought we had some fortune, and for it, had hoped to marry me—or Mary? Would he be so callous as to link himself to one not long for this world, hoping he might secure the fortune Mr Darcy denied him? The thought made me ill. But no, surely that could not be.

When the dance finished, he bowed gallantly and led us to where our party stood. After a quick pause for refreshment, he whisked Miss Darcy off to dance, leaving me with Mary and Mrs Younge.

"Mrs Younge," I asked, "how came you to know the Darcys?"

A flash in her eyes, like an animal trapped, was replaced as quickly with the easy answer of, "I worked at the school Miss Darcy attended, and left to become her companion at the request of her brother." She said nothing further, and something in her expression suggested that she did not wish to share more.

"Did you enjoy London?" I asked.

She shrugged and turned to the dancers.

Miss Darcy and Mr Wickham laughed and twirled, managing the intricate patterns with ease. They seemed so comfortable together, and I was pleased that she had a brotherly figure to entertain and adore her.

Having a brother sounded lovely. Someone protective and spirited. Someone not confined to being graceful and decorative. Someone who would help you break the rules and teach you to swim or shoot or ride a horse astride—all the sorts of things forbidden in our house as vulgar.

Mary clutched at her stomach and declared the need to return to our room, so we asked Mrs Younge to communicate our goodbyes and apologies to our aunt and uncle, and to Miss Darcy and Mr Wickham. The last thing I saw of them was him winking at her and bowing with great flourish. The affection was more pronounced than I thought proper, but having two sisters who were irrepressible flirts, I thought it was harmless.

―――

The following afternoon, I suggested to Aunt Philips that we go to tea in the hotel.

Her face soured. "Is the food any good?"

I stifled a laugh. My aunt and uncle were not known for their taste in food or fashion; they were more interested in flourish than substance.

When Mary said it was, Aunt Philips shouted for her husband and suggested we all go down for tea.

While walking to our table, I heard someone call my name, and turned to see Miss Darcy—not with Mr Wickham, but with her brother! My heart leapt, but when I noted his face remained solemn upon seeing me, my heart sank again. We paused and I made the necessary introductions, though I forced myself to maintain my reserve and was grateful my aunt and uncle likewise restrained themselves.

Fearful we would overstay our welcome, I said our table was waiting and that I hoped we might all meet again. I was not sure how sincerely my comments were meant, but I hoped that perhaps in this new venue he would be more pleasant.

CHAPTER 20

Over the next few days, Mary found herself in greater need of rest and assistance and my aunt and uncle were more interested in seeing Ramsgate than they were in tending to someone ill. Between that and their commentary on the cost of everything and their loud, vulgar gossip at the table, I wished they had delayed their arrival.

One evening, with Mary fatigued and my aunt and uncle dining at a different hotel with friends, I joined Miss Darcy for dinner. I ought to have known that Mr Darcy would be present, and endeavoured not to react when I saw him rather than Mr Wickham awaiting me. Mr Wickham had all but disappeared in the three days since Mr Darcy's arrival, and when I mentioned him, both Miss Darcy and Mr Darcy stiffened. I considered speaking of him simply to vex Mr Darcy, but did not wish to bring Miss Darcy further anxiety.

During the meal, Mr Darcy was quiet and kept his scowls to a minimum, leaving Miss Darcy to engage me in conversation. Tonight's topic was a novel she had read, and she shared all the absurd details of it with me. She was fond of a series about an adventurous young governess who found herself in danger remarkably often. I laughed at the twists in the tale, and even Mr Darcy occasionally smiled. When she reached a plot point of the heroine surviving a ride over a waterfall, however, he interrupted. "Georgiana, really, what nonsense. She would have died!"

"And yet she did not, making it great fun."

He half rolled his eyes as he cut into his meat, but there was mirth playing upon his lips. "What do you read these days, Miss Bennet?"

"Oh," I said, pausing a moment. Then I explained that I had been reading Mary's book of sermons.

"And how do you find them?"

"Tedious." His eyes flew wide, perhaps at my honesty, and I felt I ought to say more. "I wonder whether reading them is more trying than if one heard them in a church."

"In my experience that would not necessarily be the case. Many men of the cloth have no talent for public speaking."

"George would have been marvellous at making sermons," said Miss Darcy.

Mr Darcy's face grew ashen and he did not look in her direction as he said, "Mr Wickham does excel at charming compliments and trifling presumption. They are his sole talents."

His shift in mood persisted and dampened the evening, so we did not linger at the table. He agreed to a walk, and his decision to drop back as more of a chaperon than a companion suited me. After the stroll, I thanked Mr Darcy for the evening and his chaperonage.

"It is I who should thank you." His words were kind, but his jaw was set. "Georgiana has benefited from having someone young and female about. Since taking her from school, I fear she has not had success in forming friendships with other young ladies and I have wondered whether it was truly what was best for her."

Miss Darcy squeezed his arm. "You did what you thought was correct, and there have been benefits. And I have hardly considered myself lonely since leaving Pemberley. Ramsgate has been an unexpected pleasure all around."

My eyes met Mr Darcy's, and for a moment, I saw a warmth there—as if he was the man from the woods again. But just as my cheeks began to flush, he flinched, and then it was as if curtains had been drawn behind his eyes.

Even so, he said, "I agree that being here has been...unexpectedly delightful."

Silently I concurred. It had been delightful, if also a reminder of the brief amity we once shared. Now his heart was a mystery to me. We bade one another good night and parted ways. If only I had known our mutual contentment would soon be shattered.

———

The next afternoon, I was reading a letter while Mary napped. Charlotte Lucas had written to tell me of her engagement to my cousin, Mr Collins, who was also the heir of Longbourn. And now Charlotte would be the mistress of Longbourn after my father died. Heavens! Was I envious that the rooms of my childhood home would be hers? A little. Was I surprised by her engagement? More than a little, for at almost eight-and-twenty years old, I knew Charlotte believed her prospects to be slim. I confess I had rather thought so too.

Charlotte said they met in Meryton and Mr Collins had asked for her hand within two days of meeting her. I knew she feared being alone and dependent upon her parents forever, but to marry such a man as Mr Collins? From what my father had written of him, he sounded like a fool, but I would attempt to be joyful for her. She would have the home she sought, and he was kind and well-meaning, qualities that could not be attributed to all men. Oh, how I missed Charlotte. She had been my dearest friend before I had left for London, and letters were hardly the same as whispering over tea or confiding in each other during walks through the town and the meadows.

A knock at the door startled me. I hurried to it, fearful of disturbing my sister, and was most surprised to see the chambermaid I had met some days earlier. While her uniform was neat, her eyes had a wildness about them that was unusual.

"Miss Bennet, I am sorry to bother you, but..." Lowering her voice further, she said, "Well, it might not be my place, but I thought you ought to know of an agreement."

"An agreement? What kind of agreement?" I asked, unsure how anything this maid could say would have to do with me.

"Between your friend Miss Darcy and a young man—I do not know his name—but they are talking of running off together. Forgive me, it is not my business, to be sure, but..."

I gasped even as my mind began to race. What young man? Had I seen her with any male save her brother and Mr Wickham? It could not be Mr Wickham. He was like family! But who else? Had Miss Darcy been sneaking about without my knowledge of it? It was entirely possible, for I only saw her occasionally. And why would this maid choose to tell *me* such a thing?

The maid's cheeks were pink and she leant forward. "I would not share such news—my job is to be silent, of course—but Miss Darcy is so very young and it seems she would be making a mistake that could ruin her. Having heard enough talk in these halls, I know what happens with these girls and their notions about love. I was not sure who to tell. You and she seem to be friends. I hope I have not overstepped."

"No. No, I thank you kindly." I blinked at her a few times as my mind sped round and round, then remembered to reach for my reticule. "Allow me to—"

"No." She held up a hand. "I did this for no personal gain. I hope I have done right in telling, and if not, I beg you not to report me."

"I would never!" I whispered. "But allow me to give you—"

She shook her head violently and ran off, disappearing down the servants' stairs, leaving me with more questions and despising that she had brought me such news.

Mary was asleep, so after sitting a time and agonising

over what to do, I decided to set out to find Miss Darcy. I began my search in the hotel's small tearoom where ladies often gathered, but she was not there. I looked into the milliner shop which had one entrance inside the hotel, but she was not there either. Moving down the hall, I reached the gentlemen's room where men might read the paper during the day, and smoke and drink together in the evenings. Miss Darcy would not be inside, of course, but I was curious and thus paused for a moment in the doorway.

Mr Darcy was ordering something and saw me. He offered a sombre nod, and although I attempted a neutral disposition and a small curtsey in return, something in my face must have betrayed me, for he rose and approached me with haste. "Is anything the matter?"

If the maid had misheard or fabricated the story, telling Mr Darcy would be an unforgivable mistake. If the maid was correct and he went to interrogate Miss Darcy first, she might lie or run away. No, my best action was to evade. For now.

"Miss Darcy and I had agreed to spend time together this afternoon and..." I was a terrible liar. Why had I not created a story before beginning to speak? "I–" I forced a small laugh I hoped was convincing. "I forgot where she said to meet."

He fiddled with a button on his waistcoat, his eyes narrow. "This is a room for gentlemen, Miss Bennet. You will not find my sister within. You should look elsewhere." His cold tone made me shiver.

Where was the kindness I had once known? Or the smile? He showed it now so rarely—only to Miss Darcy, it seemed. And if the maid's news was correct, would he ever smile at her again? Or would he turn on her as he turned on me, becoming an angry shadow of the man we loved? No, that *she* loved. I did not love the man before me.

"She said something of being in need of a reticule," he said with a frown, "though I cannot see how she could want for more. She carries few possessions and seems to have a variety in style of beading and material."

This made me smile despite the irritation that came over me in his presence. "Need and a new reticule are often not aligned."

He nodded, but offered no smile in return. I began to take my leave when he added, "If you find her, please tell her I am expecting us to take tea together this afternoon. And she ought not to be late."

I bit my lower lip to stop myself from saying he might wish to speak to her in a more private setting. Or that it would do for him to be kinder.

As I crossed the lobby, my aunt and uncle were just entering. My aunt, whose straw cap was so overfull with ribbons and fabric flowers I wondered if it was heavy upon her head, frowned. "Lizzy! Where are you going? *Alone?*"

I had thought only of finding my friend and not of the propriety in dashing about unaccompanied. Thinking quickly, I said, "I have been with Miss Darcy and her chaperon, Mrs Younge. I forgot my reticule—foolish me!—and returned to fetch it."

"By yourself?" My uncle's fingers pressed into his belly, which had grown so large of late that a noticeable gap revealed his shirt between his waistcoat buttons. I was surprised that my aunt, so concerned with appearances, had not forced him to change garments or to purchase a new waistcoat.

"Only for a moment. As I said, they are up the street and I—"

My aunt pointed a finger at me. "Anything can happen in a moment."

"Of course," I said. "I shall hurry back to them so as not to cause any more concern." Before they could argue, I rushed past them.

While there were various shops along the way, I hoped that Miss Darcy was not in any of the many I passed in my desire to reach the one that had a reputation for the finest reticules. Indeed, as I entered, I saw her with a saleswoman who was holding up a bag with a frame that made it look like a concertina and another that was circular with feathers and a drawstring. I nearly sagged with relief as I entered the shop.

Miss Darcy threw up her hands. "I simply cannot decide."

I thought I detected a slump in the shopgirl's shoulders, and suspected that Miss Darcy had been deliberating for quite some time. "Miss Darcy! How do you do today?"

She turned, her face alit with pleasure, and beckoned me towards her. "You must help me decide which to purchase. I have preferred one and then the other for nearly an hour." The shop girl holding the bags nodded with some desperation in her eyes.

I stepped closer and took both reticules to hold them to the light. "Each is so lovely and for such different occasions."

"This is what I have been saying, have I not, Mrs Younge?"

I noticed for the first time Miss Darcy's companion in the corner. She had nodded off and startled at the sound of her name.

"Miss Bennet, which shall I choose?"

Considering the young shop girl and the effort she likely had taken with her young patron already, I said, "Purchase both. Why choose just one when you have two such delightful choices and will have many events to attend once you are out?"

Miss Darcy clapped and the shoulders of her assistant were slumped no more, replaced with a hopeful lift and a spring in her step as she went to wrap them. Miss Darcy threw her arms around me. "How lucky I am that you arrived to set everything right!"

My joy dissolved as I recalled my purpose for seeking her out. "Would it be possible for Mrs Younge to finish here and take your purchases to the hotel? I desire to speak to you alone."

"Is the matter of a serious nature?"

I nodded, and the joy that had filled her face dimmed. She turned to Mrs Younge and instructed her to return to the hotel, ignoring the woman's protests, and whisked me outside.

"We ought to speak where others cannot hear." I had no suggestion of an appropriate location, and wished again that I had planned this moment better. I then recalled a place I had walked with Mary just past the pier that seemed ignored by most. We reached the quiet spot and sat upon a bench. Had the occasion been of a less serious nature, I would have pointed out the beauty of boats coming through the mist, which had not dissipated as it usually did before midday.

"Is there something you would like to tell me of your relationship with Mr Wickham?"

She blanched but did not speak.

"Please? You must confide in me. This matter is of grave concern."

"He is a dear man." Her voice shook. "W-we have known one another all our lives."

I cocked my head, indicating that this was hardly an explanation.

She began to wring her hands. "My brother shall be ever so angry with me. I was sworn to secrecy, but I have always told my brother everything! It has been terribly difficult not to share my news."

"If you were told to keep a secret, you cannot trust that person's intentions."

Her lip trembled. "George said it would be all right. He said it would be a lark and a celebration, and that the speed of it would please my brother, who hates pomp and ceremony. Yet I fear that assessment is incorrect and this might anger him."

"What exactly are we speaking of? Does he wish to marry you?"

She looked down at her hands whose fingers were now laced together and nodded. "I love him."

I repeated, "Does he wish to *marry* you?"

"He said...elope. And then marry over the anvil."

I sucked in a sharp breath. "Miss Darcy, you know that the days of travelling alone would bring suspicion. Even if he did marry you, which is not guaranteed, your reputation would be in tatters, and it could ruin both you and your brother."

She began to sniff and tears spilled down her cheeks.

I reached out and clasped her hand. "If you do love Mr Wickham as you say you do, then convince your brother that Mr Wickham will make you a good husband. Do it properly, not in secret."

"My brother and George will not speak. I do not understand why. George says terrible things about Fitzwilliam, and while my brother does not insult George, he will not explain anything at all! I am left in the middle, loving each of them and able to speak of nothing to either." She dissolved into tears, covering her face with her hands.

I stroked her back and let her cry and cry. I felt sorry for her, yet knew I could not let things stand. Two children screamed past us, and I looked about for their caretaker, not wishing to speak until I was certain none could overhear. A man called from a distance waving them back, and the boy and girl returned to him.

As no one else was about and Miss Darcy was calmer, I said, "While I can imagine your confusion, an elopement is not the answer. You are quite young, my dear! Speak to your brother. If he consents, then marry Mr Wickham. If he does not, well then, wait until he can be convinced, and if he never can, find someone else."

Miss Darcy sniffed and pulled out a handkerchief. She dabbed her eyes and looked to the sky. "George assured me all would be well, and that my brother would grow accustomed to the idea. Somehow—" She looked at me. "Somehow, I do not believe it. George had asked me to leave this morning, but I delayed. I know I must speak to my brother, yet could not bring myself to do so. He will be angry with me, I suspect."

I resisted agreeing too eagerly, and laid my hand upon hers. "Honesty is the only way. You know this to be true."

She rose. "You will stay with me? I cannot face him alone."

Putting my arm around her waist, we rose and began to walk. The shops had no appeal to her now, and she shuffled along, her eyes fixed to the ground. I whispered reassurances in her ear and steered her around people and carts as they crossed our path. Once at the hotel, I brought us to the doorway of the men's sitting room, but Mr Darcy was no longer there. In truth, it was a relief, as he would have looked at her for only a moment before fretting and perhaps embarrassing them both with an outburst of concern. I thought to see whether he was at tea, but if he was, the same concern remained of his public reaction, so I decided it was best that we go to her apartment. "We shall send word to him to wait on you here, in your sitting room."

CHAPTER 21

We sent a note to Mr Darcy's room. His knock came mere moments later but he was not pleased to see me answer the door, if his narrowed eyes were any indication. Nevertheless, I stepped out of Miss Darcy's apartment and closed the door behind me.

"Miss Bennet? What is this?" He moved to reach past me, presumably to open Miss Darcy's door. "My sister just sent me word to come wait on her."

"I know. Sir, there is trouble. That is to say, potential trouble."

His jaw went slack and he drew back. "Of what nature?"

"Something of a serious nature has come to light. I daresay she fears telling you." I realised such words would bring to mind the worst. Mr Darcy's face paled predictably, so I added, "No one has touched or harmed her. It is of a more romantic nature, I suppose."

He reared back. "Romantic? She is just sixteen!"

"Yes, sir, and many girls of her age develop romantic

feelings." I was not sure how much more to say. "Let her explain it herself."

He pushed past me to go into the apartment where Miss Darcy sat trembling on the sofa. I entered behind him, closing the door behind me. Before we could begin to speak, it opened again. Mrs Younge, not seeing the fearsome gentleman who had walked over to the window, said, "Miss Darcy? It is time. I will send your things..."

Her voice died as she beheld Mr Darcy and me. With a foolhardy determination, Mrs Younge glared at him, then turned to Miss Darcy. "We talked about this, remember? Ignore them and come with George, who loves you more than your brother ever could."

Mr Darcy said nothing to that, but approached the lady with measured paces, thunder gathering on his brow. Then, in a cool voice, he said, "She is not going anywhere, and I suggest you get away from here before I send for the magistrate."

Something in his aspect must have persuaded Mrs Younge that he was deadly serious for quickly she slid away and sprinted down the hall, disappearing down the stairs. Just as quickly, Miss Darcy dissolved into tears.

I knelt at her feet, took her hands in mine, and looked right in her eyes. "You must explain it to him."

"What is all of this about?" Mr Darcy asked in a terrifyingly calm tone.

I squeezed her hands, which shifted her gaze to mine. I gave her the most encouraging smile that I could. "You know that telling him the truth is best. Just speak."

She took in a deep breath. "I must confess that I meant

to run away with George Wickham." She swallowed hard and added, "To elope."

"What?"

"I said—"

"I heard you! George Wickham?" The name was said as if it were poison. "Do you know what kind of man he is? An opportunist and a lout!"

Miss Darcy and I both gasped. She rose, slipping out of my grasp, and I eased off the floor and moved to her side.

Mr Darcy loomed over her. "Do you think for a moment he asked you to run off because he loves you? He wished for your fortune, nothing else."

"That is not true," she cried out, her tears beginning anew.

"I assure you it is. How could you be so foolish? How?" She began to argue but he held up his hand to silence her, though his eyes were fixed on me. "Miss Bennet, how did you get mixed up in this? Were you part of their *plan*?"

"What?" A tremor shook me. "No! I heard of it and attempted to stop it by bringing her to you. She wished to confess, her loyalty being so strong to you."

"And Mrs Younge?" He turned to his sister. "What was her part in this?"

Miss Darcy's gaze dropped. "She said she would not get paid if I did not go. I thought at first she meant paid by you for being my companion, but now I believe she meant paid by George." A pause. "Could they have arranged this?"

Brother and sister locked eyes, and then he asked, "Why would you have agreed to leave with him?"

"Because I love him."

Mr Darcy groaned. "How could you never see the bad in him?"

"And how could you never see the good?"

"Because it is pretence. He has no good in him."

I felt I had to defend her. "Mr Wickham can be quite charming, sir."

His lips curled around his teeth. "I am well aware of that fact." A pause followed during which I regretted my last comment. "I must speak to my sister. Please leave us."

His face looked pained, so I obliged, crossing to the door.

"A moment, Miss Bennet!"

Despite the tone which offended me, for I was no servant to be ordered about, I turned back.

Deep lines creased his forehead. "Need I beg for your discretion in the matter?"

"Of course not." I was, in fact, insulted that he felt the need to say this, yet I understood. "I will never breathe a word to anyone. I promise."

He stepped closer, his eyes searching my face. His own face, creased with worry a moment before, was suddenly soft, filled with wonder. "You are a good friend, Miss Bennet." He swallowed hard. "We are—that is, my sister is fortunate to have you."

We stood looking at each other for a moment before he bowed his head and I departed.

I picked my way back to my room with shaking legs. The afternoon had been so dramatic that I had not noticed the tightness in my shoulders and legs, or even my clenched fists until I was opening the door to Mary's bedchamber.

Mary lifted her head from the pillow to greet me. "You look pale. What has happened?"

"Nothing." It was not much of an answer, and her twisted lips said as much. "An encounter with Mr Darcy is all."

"You must not let that man upset you so, Lizzy. He has altogether too much power over you."

I sighed and sat on the edge of the mattress at her side. "Of course, you are correct. You are always correct."

She laughed quietly. "I never thought you would say such words to me. My illness has you in a muddle." She rested her head against the pillow. "Speaking of which, I believe it is time to return home."

"So soon? Mary, there is a concert tomorrow and another ball, not to mention—"

She laid a hand on mine. "I am not feeling well, Lizzy, and I wish to be at home."

And too well I understood what she meant. My lip began to tremble.

"No. No, Lizzy, you may not turn maudlin on me. It is a fact that I shall die, and I cannot have you sobbing over me every time I mention it."

A sob escaped my lips and I had to wipe my eyes and nose. "I have no control over myself. You have said it is my greatest weakness." I laid down in the small space between the edge of the mattress and her body, facing away from her.

She pressed her knees into the back of mine and scooted closer so her warmth ran along my back. Putting an arm around my waist, she squeezed me tight. "Have you ever wondered what it would be like to be in bed in this fashion with a man?"

I gasped. "Mary!"

"I am religious, not dead within." We giggled and she settled against me again. "There are some things I am disappointed I shall miss in this lifetime. I had hoped to marry. I had hoped to have children."

My chest tightened with pity for her.

"There was no assurance that I would have been chosen. My prospects were slim, so I admit to a modicum of relief that I shall not have to endure the true possibility of watching my four sisters find husbands whilst I became the maiden aunt left to care for Mama."

I was quiet. I suspected we all secretly hoped Mary would be the buffer between us and our aging mother.

"Mary, is there anything you wish to do that you might accomplish? Marriage seems too much to ask for, but might I arrange anything for you?"

She pressed her cheek to my back. "Ramsgate was all the adventure I could have asked for, and this time with you was precious. I am ready to go home now."

CHAPTER 22

My aunt and uncle claimed it was too soon for us to depart, as letters had to be sent and arrangements made. Mary accepted the brief delay, and while we waited three more days, we went on walks, however brief, and took tea in public, though she consumed less and less. Other meals, at Mary's request, were brought to our apartment and I kept her company. The second day we saw lines of soldiers and naval men as they marched to waiting ships. One group was in kilts, and I caught Mary looking at their legs, which made us dissolve into laughter. The last morning, despite a light rain, she asked that we walk together to the library to return our books. We stood at the windows of the library taking in every bit of the grey sea and the grey sky whose clouds rippled like waves.

Quietly, Mary said, "'Let the sea roar, and all that fills it, the world and those who dwell in it! Let the rivers clap their hands, let the hills sing for joy together before the Lord.'" She took my hand. "Amen."

"Amen," I whispered.

The journey home was arduous. Aunt and Uncle Philips spent a great deal of time listing the many things they were not able to do at Ramsgate given our early departure. Though we had first travelled without them and would have gladly returned to Longbourn in the same fashion, they would not hear of it, yet they would not be silent about the inconvenience, either.

Mary attempted to sleep as much as she could, but was frequently jolted awake by ruts in the road. By the time we reached Meryton, she was uncomfortable and peevish. Though I could see her attempts at civility, our aunt and uncle did little to ease the situation, and she became what she hated in herself: a fussy scold.

The carriage slowed in front of Longbourn, where our family and servants all awaited us. My aunt and uncle went first in a flurry of greetings and complaints and exclamations. The footman assisted me, and then we both helped Mary to navigate the coach stairs. I knew she would be horrified if her legs buckled in front of everyone, and so I held her especially tightly. She whispered her thanks and we moved towards the family. Our father approached and hugged her, taking the burden of her weight off of me. I trailed behind as he kissed her temple and brought her into the house, whispering questions and kind words.

I paused to look about. Longbourn. My home. Unlike Mary, I would marry someday and leave it, and likely not in too many years more, so for now, I thought, I would endeavour to appreciate it as I had not done in the past.

Lydia and Kitty ran to me, their questions tumbling out on top of each other such that I could scarcely discern one from the other. "How was the sea? Were there soldiers? Were they handsome? Did you attend assemblies?"

"Girls," Jane said, "let Lizzy be. The journey was long. I am sure she will tell us all about Ramsgate after she has washed and rested."

Mama came for a kiss. "We shall eat in an hour. Do ready yourself quickly, for I long to hear of any eligible men you might have met."

I smiled. Poor Mama. It was no small task to marry off five girls. No, not five. Four. I pressed my lips together to hold in my emotion and nodded.

Jane threaded her arm through my elbow, and we walked in the house. "How is Mary?" she whispered, and my crumpling face must have said all for she added, "Let us speak on it in our room."

Jane sat at the side of my bed as I washed myself and shared tales of the weeks away. It was a brief journey, but so much had happened. I told her of the ships and the pier, of the library and the shops, of buying Mary a dress and Miss Darcy's indecision over the reticule. I told her of the assembly and how Mary had danced, and how Mr Darcy had arrived and of meeting Mr Wickham.

I did not to share any of what had befallen Miss Darcy or the proposed elopement. When asked, I said Mr Darcy had been more civil to me than last time we met, though our conversations were brief. This was true. Keeping the secret from Jane was difficult, and my guts twisted at the thought of having to keep it from her forever. I was unaccustomed to having any news of my own and did not like it.

"Tell me of *here*. I have had no letters for a week. Has there been any excitement?"

"Mr Bingley has returned."

When I first arrived back in London after my disastrous meeting with Mr Darcy at the Meryton assembly, Jane had written that Mr Bingley had called and shown her attention. Then, to her surprise, he had vanished, leaving no word save a general greeting sent through his sisters.

"Mr Bingley is here again?"

"Yes, just five days ago. He is even more wonderful than I knew. I spent the day at Netherfield, and his sisters were very kind to me. Mr Bingley says he will throw a ball."

I wanted to be excited, and worked to make my face and voice match the expectations of the moment. This was wonderful news for Jane, and I hoped his return would lead to her happiness.

"You would do well to ask him to make it sooner rather than later. Once we are in mourning—" I cleared my throat. "We will be unable to attend events for a time."

The joy in my sister's expression faded, and she clasped my hands tightly as I told her of Mary's ebbing strength. A quarter hour later, when we entered the dining room, I was disappointed but not surprised to learn Mary would not join us for the meal. The conversation was light and jovial, and I did my best to participate and enjoy as was expected, but the heaviness in my heart was profound. I would need to learn to live with it and pretend to be cheerful, yet in this moment, I could not conceive of how.

"And was Mary a dreary companion?" asked Kitty, and

she and Lydia giggled, each peal of laughter stabbing at my heart.

Jane shot them each a chastening frown and I straightened in my chair. "Mary and I had a marvellous time. She is interesting and kind, and you would do well to know her before it is too late!"

The words slipped out without my thinking, and everyone stilled. Why was I not more careful? I was not wrong, but speaking such a truth aloud was not right.

My mother rose, looking ill herself. "Excuse me, I am in need of some air."

She left the room and our father followed her. Jane and I locked eyes, and I shrugged the slightest bit to show that I knew I was in error and required no further scolding. Our younger sisters said no more and ate the rest of their meals solemnly.

―――――

Mr Bingley came to call the next afternoon, which brought lightness to an otherwise miserable day. When he realised the Ramsgate party had arrived, he offered to return another day, but Mama insisted he remain, and while Jane flinched at the volume of our mother's protestation, she was smiling when he said he would be pleased to visit for a while.

We all took tea together, even Mary, who sat quietly on the sofa beside me. Although Mr Bingley seemed content in our too-crowded parlour, after a time, I suggested he and Jane go for a walk and offered to act as their chaperon if that was desired. Mary had already excused herself for a rest, and so I felt comfortable leaving the house.

The three of us stepped out the front door, Mr Bingley remarking on the mild day and Jane agreeing that it was pleasanter than expected given the grey start to it. What further conversation I overheard (for I kept a fair distance from them once we left Longbourn's gates) was not any more interesting than the exchange about the weather, but I was pleased to see Jane smile in earnest at his attention and giggle at his jokes. She tilted her head towards him when he spoke, and blushed at his compliments, of which there were many.

As we strolled to the top of the hill, I looked about the land and recalled showing Mr Darcy this view. This time, instead of musing about my insignificance, I considered all that we would have to do upon Mary's death. We would need to procure ribbons and lavender, dye our gowns (the scant week we had spent in full mourning for a great uncle we did not know had hardly taxed our wardrobes), and purchase mourning jewellery for those of us who wished it. Our mother should be the one concerned with such necessities but I knew we could not depend upon it. Making arrangements in advance of the unhappy event would ensure my sister was properly honoured in death as she was not in life.

I realised my mind had wandered too long when I looked up and discovered Mr Bingley and Jane had already descended the hill. They were far ahead of me and I had to hurry to be within a reasonable and respectable distance of them. It was not that they needed a chaperon for an open walk such as this, but Jane was always concerned with propriety. Fortunately, they seemed lost in each other's company and had not noticed that I was so far away. I hoped he would eventually offer for Jane. They seemed very well suited, and he had the financial resources to keep our family from ruin. Additionally, I thought with some shame, their union would make it possible for me to marry someone I liked rather than for wealth alone.

As we neared the house, Jane turned back and waved me closer. "Mr Bingley will host a ball in one week's time."

"How delightful," I said, attempting to sound excited.

"It need not be...sooner?" he asked.

I shook my head, which felt suddenly out of balance. "One could not plan a ball in less time than that. And even a week is brief to organise such an event. No," I gave him an encouraging smile. "I do not foresee anything standing in the way of it."

I hoped I was right. Mary seemed to know what was occurring within her but only shared part of it. A week. I hoped to have at least twice that with my sister. Why had I waited so long to see her? The *true* her?

Jane said, "Mr Bingley must return to Netherfield before dark, but desires to bid Mama and Papa farewell before he does."

"Quite right," he said.

The goodbyes at the house were prolonged by repeated kind words and hopes of seeing one another soon and of excitement about the ball. Around and around they all went in such a show of affection and civility that I soon grew peevish, slipping away to go see to the comfort of my younger sister.

"Mr Bingley could not be more perfect for Jane," Mary opined, her eyes closed and face to the ceiling.

I reached out for her hand. "I agree. I hope they shall come to an agreement soon. I cannot understand why he has not asked."

"I suspect it has to do with Mr Darcy."

"What?" I asked, instantly more alert.

"He did not seem fond of our family—any except you—when first he was our guest. Perhaps he warned his friend away from our sister, but then had a change of heart." She pulled in a laboured breath. "But what do I know of such things?"

"You are very observant, Mary."

"I had nothing to do but observe all these years, dear sister. When one is invisible, one learns a great deal." She dozed off and I slipped out of the room.

CHAPTER 23

The night of the ball, Mary was feeling poorly. In spite of Jane and Mama's protests, I chose to stay back with her.

As dawn broke, the sound of a carriage coming down the road woke me. I had fallen asleep in the parlour while waiting for my family to return from the ball. Aching, I rose, and met them at the door. They were in high spirits, even Jane, who grabbed my hand and dragged me to our room.

"Lizzy, you would not believe the night we had. I danced with Mr Bingley *twice*, and we spoke nearly any time he was not dancing, and at the end of the evening, he asked if he could call this morning. Dare I believe—? Oh Lizzy, could he be wanting my hand in marriage?"

"It would be wonderful if so."

I helped her out of her gown and removed pin after pin from her hair, asking about the food and the musicians, and whether his sisters had been present. I chose not to ask about anyone else.

"Mr Darcy was there," she said, as if she could read my mind. "He asked after you."

"Oh?" I strove to keep my voice light, unconcerned.

"He seemed disappointed that you had remained at home," she said, hastening to add, "although he understood your reasons. Perhaps he will call with Mr Bingley later this morning."

I shrugged and slid into bed.

In fact, Mr Darcy did accompany Mr Bingley, but only to deliver his friend to our door. I watched from my bedchamber window as the two men conversed briefly. Mr Darcy seemed to be speaking to him sternly. At first, I wondered whether he was encouraging or discouraging Mr Bingley from knocking. It was difficult to tell, but then Mr Darcy walked to the door himself, rapped hard upon it, and spoke some final words at Mr Bingley before marching away. Remarkably, Mr Darcy disappeared into the woods where he and I been when Mr Goulding arrived at Longbourn. Why would he go there? Much as I was tempted to follow him and ask, I knew I had to forget about him; he had long ago forgotten about me.

Jane was already in the parlour. I hastened to join her but as I arrived, Mama was hurrying the family out. Papa was to wait in his study, where, if the conversation went as everyone hoped, Mr Bingley might ask permission to marry dear Jane.

Remarkably—for what in life ever occurs as hoped for and planned—within minutes, that is precisely what occurred. My mother shrieked and Jane beamed; Papa smiled and Mr Bingley quaked. I hoped he shook with delight but realised it was likely relief as much as anything. All returned to the parlour, calling for servants who were, surprisingly, nowhere to be seen.

I decided to run upstairs myself to tell Mary the news and found Hill standing on the landing weeping quietly. As I approached, she straightened.

"I am sorry, Miss Lizzy." She wiped her cheeks quickly with her handkerchief.

I collapsed onto the stairs, whispering, "Oh, no. No, not— Oh, Mary." I could feel a wail forming in my throat, but I did not wish to ruin Jane's moment of pure happiness, and told Mrs Hill so.

She agreed and so for a time I sat in lonely desolation, hearing the celebration below and bracing myself for all that was to come.

———

That afternoon, the sight of the black tea set stopped me mid-stride as I entered the parlour. It ought not to have. We had used it in the past when our great uncle died, but this was different. It was for *Mary* that all decoration had been stripped from our world.

My mother was staring at the pot as if it were a monster that might attack, so I reached out and poured. No one else was interested, so I took the cup and sipped, staring out the window. The temptation to be away from the rest of my family, to mourn in private, was suddenly too much to be denied and with the fewest syllables possible, I excused myself from the room and was soon striding through the woods.

A noise in the underbrush at one particular point in

the path made me jump, but when I looked about, I saw nothing. Probably just a woodland creature searching for food.

I took a seat on a fallen log once I had reached a secluded enough place. Closing my eyes, I listened, hearing nothing more than birds twittering overhead. Mary would have liked the sound, though not the damp from the log that was seeping into my dress. I endeavoured to let myself drift away, for this world was too painful.

"Miss Elizabeth?"

I scrambled to my feet, my heart pounding. "Who is there?"

Mr Darcy stepped from behind a tree. "I am sorry. I-I was walking and heard a noise, and once I realised it was you, I knew you would wish to be alone, but could not escape without revealing myself." He bowed. "Forgive this intrusion."

I smoothed my skirt. "I..." But I could think of nothing to say.

"I received the news of your sister's death. I am so very sorry." His brows knit together. "I know how difficult it can be to endure such a loss."

I recalled his devastation when he learnt of his own brother's death, how he blanched and then wept. But had it been agony over the brother or for the responsibility that came with his brother's death that tore at Mr Darcy? I thought it was more the latter, but he knew grief and I was in need of a confessor.

I took a step towards him. "I have so much guilt. Why did I not spend time with her when we were younger?

Why did I not speak to her every day and love her better? For too long, I treated her as an annoyance, not realising how wonderful she was, and now she has departed this world and I-I wasted it!"

Our eyes locked in the silence, and a warmth spread over me that took me by surprise.

He took a step closer, yet the distance between us was still vast. "You are fortunate to own such loving feelings for her, even if they came late. You treated your sister with great kindness in Ramsgate." He looked away and sighed heavily. His head drooped. "My guilt is in never finding anything I enjoyed about Thomas. It pains me and always shall."

"You cannot create affection where there is none."

"No." He pulled in a long breath before lifting his head. "Speaking of affection, are you pleased with the match between Bingley and Miss Bennet?"

"In that she is happy, very much so." I forced myself to speak the name of my other beloved sister. "Mary suggested it was you who brought them together in the end, but that it had also been you who dissuaded Mr Bingley's initial proposal."

His eyes widened.

I said, "Mary was perceptive."

Mr Darcy ran his fingers through his thick dark hair—hair I had run my own fingers through years ago near this very spot. His eyes locked on mine. "I did have grave concerns about Mr Bingley joining himself to your family."

"My family?"

He nodded, his brow furrowed. His eyes searched my

face and he opened his mouth as if to say something, but then clapped it shut.

My heart thrummed all the while as I wondered what he wished to say about my family. About me. The silence dragged on, so I said, "One cannot choose one's relations."

He nodded again but said nothing more, which set me to talking.

"I find them maddening and yet I bear affection for them. They are all I have, and I must rely on them for all that I need and desire. I have no means to support myself, no ability to strike out on my own as a young man might, and no one with whom I might live in town." I could not stop speaking, though I knew I should. "My aunt and uncle Philips are crude, even by my estimation. I know you would loathe them. They were at Ramsgate at the end, which was unpleasant, but happily you met but once. I believe I am no longer welcome with my aunt and uncle Gardiner, as I required them to watch me more closely than they would have liked when I stayed with them last in town."

I felt more like weeping as each set of relatives filled my mind. "In order to refrain from being anyone's burden, I shall live here at Longbourn, wishing for an escape and knowing perfectly well that my only hope is to marry. I pray it is to a man I do not despise and who does not despise me, though the prospect of any union—even a horrible one—fades with every passing year. Mary made her peace with being a spinster, but I cannot."

To hide from my own humiliation, I looked away. "You should leave me to my grief, Mr Darcy," I said, as if that would explain the appalling barrage of truth I had just shared.

When he did not move or speak, I turned back to him, dreading to see the pity on his countenance. But rather than pity, was it affection that I saw? Without thinking, I stepped forward, closing the distance between us. A shiver ran through me. These woods. This man. This longing. This desire. Every time I thought these feelings had been wholly banished, they returned.

I could confess that I never forgot about our days in these woods. That I would give anything to entwine my limbs with his, to press my lips to his neck. Oh, what I did not wish to do!

He began to lean in, and I thought for sure he would kiss me. It seemed natural to reach towards him, or it did until he froze and stepped back, his eyes wide with horror.

My hands fell to my sides. Where moments earlier hurt and humility had softened his features to those I had once known, now the too-familiar frown had set back upon his brow. Hurriedly, I tucked my arms behind my back, clasping my hands together behind me.

When he spoke, his voice had grown cold. "I *did* attempt to stop the union between Bingley and your sister. He is expected to raise himself in society through his choice of a wife."

My longing dissipated, replaced quickly by irritation. "Mr Bingley's family made their money in trade. My father was born—"

"And yes, the manners of your family..." He rocked back on his heels, and I thought—nay, hoped—he might cease speaking, but he did not. "They displayed a total want of propriety so frequently, so almost uniformly, save you and Miss Bennet."

I blinked rapidly a few times, as if that might erase his cruel words.

"Forgive me," he said, his voice softer. "Given the situation with your sister, I ought not—" He winced and began to back away.

An odd calm settled over me. "I perfectly comprehend your feelings, and have now only to be ashamed for what my own have been."

"*Your* feelings?"

"When you visited my family all those years ago, I believed us to be amiable companions who might have a future with one another. I held a hope of you, but had not comprehended how loathsome we all were in your eyes."

"Not *all*."

"I wonder now why I ever believed that ours would be a fortunate match when, once the first days of our acquaintance had ended, you were nothing but cold to me...even outright rude at times. It would be madness to spend more time with you than is required given my desire for a happy life! I am bound to my family, troubling as they might be."

He bit back his reply as if pained by whatever he wished to say. Finally, in a low voice, he said, "You could remove yourself from them."

At this I laughed. But it was an angry laugh. "*Your* family made you miserable, and continue to do so from the grave! Yet you advise *me*? Sir, you have stepped beyond all reasonable propriety. And unlike you, and despite their countless faults, I love my family."

"I love my sister."

"May God protect her from your judgment."

His jaw clenched tightly. He spun and disappeared into the woods.

I sank back down on my log and wept.

CHAPTER 24

Two days later, mourners filled Longbourn. Mary would have found it laughable that so many people who overlooked her in life came to acknowledge her in death, even though she had predicted as much.

While the men were at the church, many ladies milled about the house, speaking in soft tones and approaching me with condolences. Jane received low whispers of congratulations, and she thanked them just as quietly. It had been unfortunate timing becoming engaged the very same morning that her sister died. After the service, Mr Bingley returned and escorted Jane into the sitting room to speak for a time, for which I was glad. He would be a comfort to her.

Miss Caroline Bingley was on the arm of Mr Darcy as they stood near the refreshments. She held herself with the same imperiousness I recalled from the assembly some months back, and he appeared grave and uncomfortable. She leant in to talk to him, pressing her fingers into his arm, and I had to look away.

I took hold of my shawl and drifted out to the garden and past the gates, sitting on a stump with my face to the sky. I shivered from the cold but did not desire to return to the house. It ought not to have been sunny on a day like this. Where was the autumn rain to match my melancholy?

"Miss Elizabeth?"

I turned, and to my dismay, Mr Darcy stood before me. "I have no will to argue or to be censured, Mr Darcy. Please leave me be."

"I came to pay my respects."

"Respects?" I sprang to my feet. "You have no respect for me or my family."

He winced.

"Forgive me." I took a slow breath. "It would be best if I were alone."

He frowned but much to my despair, he did not leave. I could not withstand more insults or, worse, his sympathy. He knew too well my family's foibles and I had shared too freely my true feelings about all of them. My shame was agonising.

"I desire to speak to you on another matter."

I searched for more impertinent words, but could think of none. I nodded, my vision blurred with fury.

"I have a proposal for you."

I froze.

"My sister is in need of minding. She says she is mature and capable, but—" He looked over his shoulder, likely to ensure that we were alone "—as we know from recent events, her judgment cannot be trusted. You are in need of a house in which to seek refuge and solace—a place to heal, and a point from which to have adventures. I am certain your spirits languish in a place such as Meryton."

Before I could fully take offence, he said, "Georgiana similarly claims her spirits wither at Pemberley. Young women ought not to be isolated, and London—though I find it generally abhorrent—pleases many with its cultural and social opportunities. After the troubles with Mrs Younge, I find it difficult to trust anyone, but I would trust you with my dear sister's reputation. Nay, her life. You have proved yourself to be beyond reproach."

I thought of our time together at Ramsgate. Miss Darcy was such a dear. I was pleased to have been of service to the family and I understood the impulse to do anything to secure her happiness. Mr Darcy had almost been kind in those moments, and I knew he was grateful for my intervention with Mr Wickham.

"What, pray, are you asking of me, sir?"

"My sister wishes to have her coming out ball next spring. I have no interest in planning it, nor, I suspect, talent for such matters. She is in want of close female relations, and as she admires you deeply, she asked whether you might help her plan the event."

A ball? Me? I had never planned any such occasion, and had only even attended a few. Certainly the events held in and around Meryton were nothing to what was seen in town.

"As this is occurring," he continued, "you could live at our Grosvenor Street home. Georgiana would love no companion more than you. In fact, she requested that I ask this favour of you. I must be at Pemberley, and our lands in Scotland need attending, so I would be entirely absent for the next many months. I had dismissed the idea until our conversation yesterday."

I sat straighter, as if that show of pride might erase my humiliation of the day prior. "I have every plan to live happily at Longbourn."

"I understand that feeling of deep misery and hopelessness. I have had to force myself to wake and face each day since my parents' deaths, and dread nearly every task before me. Living in a constant state of despair is the worst pain imaginable, so if I can save you from such agony and help my sister simultaneously, then I am glad to do so."

I felt sorrier for him than I ever had. 'Worst pain? Agony? Dread?' Is this how he passed his days? No wonder he was so gruff and uncompromising.

I rose, wishing I could throw my arms around him and comfort him. "Mr Darcy, if you are truly so unhappy, then change your life. Make it a life you are pleased by."

He shook his head. "I cannot. I am trapped, with no means of escape. But I desire to assist you and save you from a similar fate of helplessness." His eyes darkened and he began to plead with me. "Do not marry rashly. Do not stay in Meryton, a town lacking diversions, sophisticated society, and culture. You are too lively to be held prisoner by circumstance. I beg of you to be Georgiana's companion."

His sudden and unexpected request was too much to comprehend. While it was appealing—I could live in London and not be a burden to my family—I would be beholden to a man who churned my emotions more than anyone I knew. It was madness—he made me angry, sad, frustrated, and seemed loath to be near me. Why would he help me? Was it solely out of care for his sister?

"So, you wish for me to be in your *employ*?"

"Not my employ, no. I do not know what to call it, but the situation is as stated. You would be her guest and have a home. I would be elsewhere. You could be free, and I would be grateful to you."

What a strange turn of events!

"I must think on it."

"Of course. Of course." He pulled at his waistcoat. "Might you tell me on the morrow, as I hope to return to Pemberley and give Georgiana your decision, whatever it may be, as soon as possible?"

I nodded and he bowed, leaving me with many questions. Was Mr Darcy as melancholy as he claimed? What could be done to assist him? Was it my place to try?

Later that afternoon, Jane and I escorted Kitty and Lydia on a walk in an attempt to check their behaviour and to keep them from Meryton. We looked like crows in our black gowns, and more than once the younger girls despaired, saying that black made their complexions appear sickly. "Jane," I asked as the others picked flowers on the side of the path, "have you given thought to the wedding?"

She shook her head. "Mr Bingley suggested we plan for three months from Mary's death, but I believe we need more time, and Mama and Papa ought to wait six months before attending a celebration."

Six months. Would that mean half a year before I could go to town with Miss Darcy? It would be right to wait until after the wedding to begin my own adventure, to support and help Jane plan, but now that the idea was in my head, I wished to run away from Longbourn as soon as possible. As Mr Darcy had said, I felt trapped and it made every bit of me ache.

Was this the pain Mr Darcy was enduring? Did that excuse his behaviour? I had to cease thinking of him as it only deepened my heartache.

"Dearest, begin your happy new chapter with haste. Set the date for three months hence, just after the new year, if Mama and Papa will allow it."

Was I speaking in her interest or my own?

CHAPTER 25

May 1812, London

Everything was in place. The chandeliers sparkled. The eight-hour length wax candles were all lit with more out of sight to replace those that burnt low—an extravagance to which I could never grow accustomed.

The mirrors that festooned the ballroom and halls and music room had been polished and polished and polished again, as were the candelabras and silverware. I noticed how the servants' hands reddened at the task, and though I was not meant to consider them, I had never found a way not to. More maids and servants had been hired for preparations for Miss Darcy's ball, meaning the top floor of the house was temporarily overrun. For the past three nights, I had heard giggles in the evening from above, and while a true mistress of a house (which I was not) might object to such intrusion, I was glad for their merriment.

Sixty sweet and savoury dishes awaited the guests, who would be served supper at approximately eleven o'clock, and would be laid out carefully on a table that stretched the length of the ballroom. Punch, filling the largest bowls I had ever seen, waited on each end of the table, and additional ice rested in storage should it be needed. Flowers festooned every surface. Incredibly, for I had not been to any balls this extravagant, artists had been hired to draw chalk pictures on the floor. When I argued that the images would be ruined, I was told that the chalk had a double purpose: in addition to their beauty, they would keep the dancers from slipping on the highly polished floor. Before the guests arrived, I took one last admiring look at the lovely depictions of pastoral scenes.

The musicians were uncharacteristically early, for they had been paid extra to arrive in a timely fashion so as not to add anxiety. Yes, Miss Darcy would be at ease—or at least as close to at ease as a girl in her position could be. She was shy, but knew her duty and did thrill at the idea of a party entirely in her honour.

In January, Jane had been equally reluctant to be the centre of attention, though her wedding had made her excessively happy in the end. Oh! How I missed my dear sister just now. Jane's wedding breakfast had been lavish for a country affair. Bingley's servants had arranged much of it, as Jane had hesitated to plan, feeling it was disrespectful to Mary's memory. Besides, the event was at Netherfield since our servants were too few and our rooms too small for an event the size Bingley desired.

On the day of her wedding, Jane had been full of quiet mirth and reserved celebration. Her shy smile had lifted the spirits of all who gazed on her, and her calm affection made Bingley glow. Though I abandoned her for London the day after, her letters arrived weekly to the Grosvenor Street house, and her tales of marital felicity put me at ease.

Save for Bingley and Jane, my family was not invited to Miss Darcy's ball. I was relieved that even Jane would not be able to travel, as she was expecting already, which would lessen the slight to the others. Miss Darcy had suggested all be asked, but I declined. Despite my twinges of guilt, I could not subject myself or her guests to my family's behaviour. Or my family to Mr Darcy's scrutiny.

At Jane's wedding, Lydia and Kitty had commented loudly on the sipping chocolate and quality of the food, and Mama walked about telling all who would listen that the marriage was inevitable as Jane had been fated for a good match given her beauty. No attempts to control their comments quieted them, and the thought of being embarrassed again overwhelmed me. My relations were not of the Darcys' circle, and the inclusion of them might only invite ridicule and speculation. Or so I told myself. I was a coward.

And now, after months of planning and discussion, the event was, at last, upon us. Having checked that all was ready, I went up to gather Miss Darcy.

After knocking, I entered her room and found her with her maid, Miss Mitchell, at the dressing table.

"Shall I use the white flowers, or the pink?" Miss Darcy, having bathed in hot water followed by cool to improve her complexion, having been rubbed with lotions and puffed with powders, was now addressing her hair. The curling papers had been removed, and her blonde tresses were elaborately twisted and pulled into a shape that flattered her face—the perfect combination of soft and slim.

"Both?" I suggested, and she rolled her eyes. I had been attentive for months about the preparations, but I had at last grown weary of decisions. I approached her and rested a hand on her shoulder, saying to Miss Mitchell, "Pink, in contrast with the gown."

Miss Darcy and I had enjoyed days at the modiste picking out the cut and fabrics and trimmings for her gown. Unlike Mary, Miss Darcy enjoyed the details, if not always the attention. The proprietor, Mrs Thomas, had greeted us warmly and led Miss Darcy through the decision-making process with patience and care. The white satin was nearly the colour of Miss Darcy's skin, and the laces and ribbons highlighted her youth perfectly.

Miss Darcy insisted that I acquire a gown at her cost, and after multiple refusals I agreed, choosing one in pale lavender. I was observing half mourning for my sister, though this was not required of me, and chose the colour as a reminder of dear Mary. However, I selected a fabric with shine so as to mask the nod to my loss. My gown was simpler than Miss Darcy's, but I did believe I looked fine in it and thanked her as we admired ourselves in our new acquisitions.

With the last bloom fastened in place, Miss Darcy rose. Miss Mitchell clasped her hands together. "Miss Darcy, you look more beautiful than anyone I've ever seen."

Miss Darcy leant in to kiss Miss Mitchell on the cheek and whispered, "Try to peek in a few times if you can."

Once downstairs, Miss Darcy gasped at the sight of the

decorated rooms. "Have you ever seen anything so lovely?"

"The room is not as lovely as you," said a voice and we both spun to find Mr Darcy beaming at his sister. She ran to him and squeezed him around the middle as she must have been doing since she was young. It was endearing to see this moment of familial affection.

Mr Darcy had arrived a mere three hours earlier. I had heard the carriage pulling up and his man barking orders to the footman for the things required to ready his master for the evening. Letters had arrived in the days prior announcing his delay—first due to a flood at the Scotland property and the second sending regrets due to a broken axle that delayed him further. He had assured Miss Darcy that he would not miss the event even if it meant he would ride a mule or an ox to London. I would like to have had the opportunity to see that, and chuckled occasionally at the thought, but, alas, the repair was completed in time.

The bell rang, and Bingley, the first guest, entered without my sister, as planned. We greeted each other warmly and after assuring me that Jane was well, he complimented Miss Darcy, then me, then the house. Another guest entered, and another, and the much-anticipated event was on its way to becoming a happy memory.

Mrs Lambert arrived with her husband—she was aglow with new motherhood and the freedom of an evening out. Though we ought not to have neglected the other guests, she and I stole into a corner to share confidences until her husband came to gather us like naughty school children. He desired to dance with Mrs Lambert, and against her protests I urged her to go, arguing that I ought to speak to the butler and be certain that all was well with the food, soon to be laid out.

As I moved to the other end of the ballroom, noticing the loveliness of the music, I spotted Mr Darcy. On his arm was a woman with chestnut hair and skin so pale it seemed translucent. Her hair was pinned neatly in the latest fashion, and her gown seemed to float about her figure as if held by angels. Guests greeted them, and while Mr Darcy nodded and spoke, the woman merely stared.

Eventually they made their way to where I stood rooted to the spot. "Miss Elizabeth Bennet," he said, "may I present Miss Lavinia Vane."

Her head moved the slightest bit, and I suspected that was meant to be a nod.

"Miss Vane and I met on the Highlands when we were children. Her family has an estate near ours in Scotland."

Miss Vane blinked slowly in confirmation of this fact. I asked, "Do you enjoy Scotland, Miss Vane?"

A small sigh was her only response.

Attempting not to laugh at her lassitude, I asked, "How do you fill your time in Scotland?"

"Riding." A pause. "Walking." Another pause, this one so lengthy I thought to ask another question, but then she added, "Petting my corgis."

I waited for additional information, but none seemed forthcoming, and she did not ask any questions of me. The silence hung between us like a fog, and I looked to Mr Darcy to see if he found her as dull as I, but his face was impassive.

At last, she pursed her lips and said, "Mr Darcy, I am in need of refreshment."

"Of course," he said, "but first, let us spend a moment with Miss Bennet. She planned this ball, after all."

"You are a servant?"

I nearly laughed, for her tone was so entirely droll it was nearly a parody of a woman of the *ton*. "No. I have been Miss Darcy's companion these past months and assisted, as she has no mother or sister who might serve in this capacity. But I am not employed."

"Oh yes," she said, her mouth hardly moving. "How good of you."

Yet 'good' sounded anything but. More like horse manure had just been cleaned off of her favourite riding boots.

Mr Darcy said, "Miss Vane, I have explained that Miss Bennet is a friend of the family. And by the look of this ball, she is quite talented at planning gatherings."

My cheeks burnt, and I wanted to thank him, but Miss Vane said, "Mr Darcy, you know I remember little that is of no import."

Again, I battled back laughter, though I am sure Mr Darcy caught the sparkle in my eyes, which I could not dim. "What *is* of import to you, Miss Vane?" he asked.

She sighed. "My dogs."

I grew more fixated with each word she spoke on the fact that her face did not move. A silence stretched on, and I wondered whether she was still considering Mr Darcy's question, or if she had forgotten the conversation entirely.

"My horses," she added at last.

Mr Darcy cleared his throat. "You care for Wolfshire."

Remarkably, despite not appearing to move one feature, it was clear she was displeased. "My family estate in Scotland is an abomination. Crumbling walls. Leaking roof. Nearly everything within is ruined."

The steward approached and whispered something to Mr Darcy, who apologised before disappearing with the man, leaving me alone with Miss Vane.

As if nothing had occurred, she continued. "The neglect my grandparents allowed at Wolfshire is inexcusable."

I asked, "And your parents?"

"Dead. Like Mr Darcy's." Her voice was as emotionless as her features, and I wondered how long she had been an orphan, but dared—or cared—not to ask. "It is a fact that brought us together. That and an interest in improving our ancestral lands."

"Once you repair the structure of Wolfshire," I asked, "will you fill it with art and books?"

"I care nothing for art, so I shall rely on Mr Darcy to advise me. As for books, I do not waste my time with those, either."

"Mr Darcy adores reading." I could not help myself and asked, "Does he still enjoy poetry?"

"Reading of all sorts. It is what fills his hours when we are apart," she said. "And some when we are together. Often, we have nothing to say, and so he reads."

I could not help but ask, "And what do *you* do in these moments?"

"Stare at Mr Darcy. He is handsome. Sometimes I gaze at the walls or out the window, though the view does become dull after a time." There was a pause, one which I would not break, for I was mesmerised by the amount of time it took her to share a thought. "My aunt, who is my constant companion, sometimes tells an amusing story, though I have heard most of her anecdotes many times over."

"How—" Did I wish to know the answer to this? "How often have you visited with Mr Darcy these past months?"

"Frequently." Suddenly her gaze sharpened a little. "I am expecting a proposal."

I nearly gasped, but managed to contain myself. He could not marry *her*. He *would* not. Or would he?

"I suspect it shall come soon," she said. "I see no obstacle to it. It would be advantageous to combine our fortunes, and our land, and we like each other well enough."

Well enough? Well enough! How could each of them settle for simply 'well enough'? I knew many married with even less regard for one another, but I could not imagine it for myself or for Mr Darcy. He was too alive. Too interesting. Too interested in the world.

Or he *had* been.

The man I had known these past few years was a shadow of the man I first met, and yet there were traces of that liveliness still in him. How could he so thoroughly abandon hope for joy in his life by attaching himself to Miss Vane?

Now I could no longer be entertained by her silences—dull, disinterested silences that Mr Darcy would endure for the rest of his life. No! This was untenable. I offered my good wishes, though I meant none of them, and she drifted away, leaving me sour.

At that moment, Miss Darcy hurried to my side and leant close. "My brother cannot marry her!" she hissed.

I looked about to see who might be listening, but all appeared engaged in their own conversations, so I said as low as I could over the music, "He can if he so desires. As a man, he may choose whom and when to marry."

"I cannot tolerate her! I never have. How can *he*?"

"Miss Darcy, this is your party. Do not fret about this now, just enjoy yourself."

"It is all I can think of! He told me his plan as he passed me a cup of punch as if it were of no more import than the purchase of a steed."

Hearing this—that it was his plan—made me swallow hard with disappointment. "Let us step outside for a moment to speak."

We hurried outside into the cool spring air, which I hoped would bring her back to her senses. Once at the rail, amidst the sounds of the passing carriages on the street and the din of the party, I said, "Put these matters aside. This is your celebration!"

"I cannot enjoy myself knowing that every moment following shall be a misery due to Miss Vane! If only our parents were here!"

"What would they think?"

Her head dropped and she laughed. "In fact, I believe they might adore the idea. They loved Miss Vane, though *why* I could never say!" She threw up her hands. "I have no sensible argument against her, and he would not listen if I did."

"Might I ask... What was your mother like?"

"Mother was cold and spiteful. Forgive my candour."

Only after I reassured her that I preferred truth did she continue. "I do not mean to be unkind, but I do not recall my mother having a kind word to say about anyone, other than myself and Thomas."

"And Mr Darcy?"

She shook her head. "She criticised Fitzwilliam at every turn. I could not understand it, for he was so good and thoughtful and kind. I believe it is what she hated about him."

Seeing her consternation, I reached for her arm, giving a squeeze. I was at a loss to understand how a mother could hate her son.

"Would he truly marry *her*?" she asked. "Is he seeking a wife who treats him as poorly as Mother once did? Why would he do such a thing?"

I shrugged. "I suspect he feels in need of a wife. Unlike Miss Bingley, Miss Vane is not cruel. She is simply..." I could not find the worlds. "Perhaps a lack of cruelty is all he requires in a mate."

"It ought not to be. He ought to be with someone like you."

I blanched. This course of conversation would not do, but I would speak lightly about a topic that somehow still pained me. "I cannot speak of my own qualities but from what I have seen, women who are clever and kind and have the sort of fortune and connexions he is determined to marry are as rare as well-written books."

"Indeed. Miss Vane would not know, since she never reads!"

We fell into each other, laughing.

"Speaking of connexions, we must return to the party

and begin the chore—or is it the joy?—of finding you a husband!"

I said it lightly. She had wanted to be out, though she was rather young, but Mr Darcy told her he could not countenance an engagement until she was at least eighteen.

And me? Who would I marry? Where might I find a husband who would banish Mr Darcy from my thoughts forever, and when? No. My duty was to pour my energy into Miss Darcy, at least for a few hours more. What came after that, I knew not.

"Come," I said, looping my arm through hers. "Let us see what delights await us inside."

CHAPTER 26

As we entered the over-heated ballroom, Mr Darcy approached with two young men. "Georgiana, allow me to present these gentlemen to you. This is Mr William Bexley and his brother, Mr Alexander Bexley. Gentlemen, my sister, Miss Georgiana Darcy."

She curtseyed and lowered her head, but looked at them from under her brow.

"And this is her friend, Miss Elizabeth Bennet."

"Miss Darcy," said the first Mr Bexley. "Might I have the next dance?" She agreed, and the young man's cheeks pinkened.

His brother bowed to me. He was slim with light brown hair, arresting ice-blue eyes, and a smile dancing at the corners of his lips. "Miss Bennet, might I also have the next dance?"

I agreed, and glanced at Mr Darcy. I suspected he knew this would happen. He had Miss Vane to attend to, and if both Miss Darcy and I were dancing, he was free to be with her. The thought gave my heart an involuntary squeeze.

Mr Alexander Bexley was an amiable dance partner. He knew the steps and kept the conversation lively, happily speaking beyond the weather and the delightful notes playing. As we swung into formation with Miss Darcy and Mr Bexley, he suggested we might all go to a museum soon. Miss Darcy agreed immediately, so I nodded. With the planning of the ball complete, what else were we to do? He seemed good company, and the rakish tilt of his head did set my heart galloping more than once. Perhaps there were new joys to be had in London after all.

When the dance had reached its end, the Bexleys bowed and Mr William Bexley asked if three days hence might be suitable for our museum adventure. Miss Darcy looked to me, hopeful, and I agreed.

Mr Alexander Bexley said, "We shall drive in our carriage, if that is amenable to you both," and when I nodded, the plans were set so they bowed and vanished into the sea of guests.

Before Miss Darcy and I could exchange words about the men or the dance, she was tapped on the shoulder. She spun then squealed, throwing her arms about a gentleman who looked vaguely familiar. Since Mr Darcy, who was at the man's shoulder, merely smiled, I suspected they were all friends. Nay, relatives! Now I remembered him. This was Colonel Fitzwilliam, the young man who had accompanied Mr Darcy on his travels when first we met.

"Dear Georgiana," he was saying, "my deepest apologies for our tardiness. I thought our ship would have arrived earlier, but there were delays, and I do not move as quickly as I once did." He held up a cane, and I realised it was not merely a walking stick he used to appear grander, but which he relied upon. Had he been injured in the war?

I was brimming with questions when Miss Darcy said, "Miss Bennet, this is my cousin—"

"Colonel Fitzwilliam," I interrupted. "We met some years ago."

After a slight pause, his face brightened. "Miss Elizabeth Bennet! Of course. Darcy has shared many times since we first met—"

"Tell her of your news," interrupted Mr Darcy, and I noted how flushed his cheeks were. Was it the heat of the room or something else? What had he had shared with his cousin?

Colonel Fitzwilliam reached out and eased a lovely young woman to his side. "I would like to present Miss Dorothea Turner."

She swatted at him playfully. "*Mrs* Dorothea *Fitzwilliam*, if you please."

He cackled. "Yes! My mind gets muddled with the pain." He lifted up his cane again by way of explanation. "Mrs Dorothea Fitzwilliam, my wife!"

Miss Darcy squealed. "You are married?"

"Yes," he said, kissing Mrs Fitzwilliam on the cheek. She looked at him with all the adoration I hoped to one day feel and receive. "We married on the voyage to England."

Miss Darcy asked, "You married on a ship? How romantic!"

Mr Darcy's face was grave, and I hoped he would not ruin the couple's moment of celebration.

"How did you meet?" I asked.

"She was my nurse."

Mrs Fitzwilliam's eyes drifted to Mr Darcy, and while her smile never faltered, she explained directly to him, "And lest you think I am an opportunist or a pauper, my family has land in Sussex. I ran off for adventure and to have a purpose, and I found a husband." Her eyes met mine. "My mother will at last be able to breathe."

At this I laughed aloud, imagining the dramatics if I announced that I would be venturing across the sea to be near a war, unmarried and untethered.

Miss Darcy asked, "So you met on the ship?"

"No," answered Colonel Fitzwilliam, "she was a battlefield nurse who helped me during the months of my recovery, but agreed to return with me."

"It was past time," she said, "having been abroad for three years. Too much sadness and death have dampened my spirits." In the short moments we had been together, her blue eyes had been lively and her face bright, so I wondered how much more being home could cheer her, but shuddered to think of days filled with bloodshed and suffering. "And now, I return a married woman with a wonderful match."

Colonel Fitzwilliam lifted her hand and kissed her knuckles, then turned his attention to his young cousin. "Georgiana, tell me about your splendid ball. How did you manage to plan all this? I know your brother could not have done it on his own, and with my mother occupied at Matlock with the earl's health..."

Miss Vane, whom I had forgotten was near, said, "I know this tale, Mr Darcy, and I am in need of refreshment."

Her cool voice sliced through me. Some people, like cheese or wine, improved with time, but Miss Vane was more like fish left in the sun.

"Of course." He bowed, extended an elbow, and they drifted off. Colonel Fitzwilliam's lips curled almost imperceptibly watching them leave.

Miss Darcy said, "Miss Bennet planned the ball. She is talented beyond imagining, and has been a dear companion these past months."

Mrs Fitzwilliam asked details of the dress and the musicians and the flowers, then the colonel asked after my family. I answered sparingly, taking special care not to admit my shame at not having seen my parents and sisters in so very long nor to tell them about Mary, as the evening was meant to be joyful. Even so, I felt my own discomfort rising. Perhaps he felt it, as well, for he said, "Ladies, if it shall not offend, I would like to dance with my wife before the festivities come to an end."

Mrs Fitzwilliam's delicate brow drew down. "With your leg, I do not think—"

"How else can I show you off? We need not dance the entire dance. Let us try a few minutes and see whether I can manage."

As they departed, the words, "Miss Darcy," came from behind my shoulder. I turned to see Mr William Bexley, his face full of excited expectation. "I was wondering if I might have this dance."

A second dance with Mr Bexley? It was not unheard of,

but at her own ball, she ought to have been sharing dances with a variety of eligible men. Additionally, she and I had decided she would rest and greet guests during this particular set, though I suspected Miss Darcy had told Mr Bexley that this dance had been left open and both were thrilled at the opportunity to take advantage of this fact.

I nodded when she looked to me, for what else was I—not her mother, not even a protective elder sister—to do? The couple strode away beaming. I decided to be certain supper was ready. In the dining room, I looked at the table laden with covered hot dishes and uncovered sweets, thrilled by the sight. I did not think the servants could make it possible, yet all was here, and even finer than at Jane's wedding. I moved towards the housekeeper to thank her, but she was slipping through the door to the servants' stairs, leaving me with the butler, Mr Clarke, who appeared surprised by my effusive thanks. One servant I did not recognise looked up from setting a platter when Mr Clarke said, "It is our job, Miss Bennet."

I stepped back to allow a footman on loan from a neighbouring house past. "Indeed sir, but not all accomplish their duties with such aplomb, so I thank you heartily, and I know Miss Darcy is very pleased."

The expression that slid across his face could not be considered a smile, but it approximated appreciation, so I felt satisfied, and watched him alert the guests to the readiness of the meal.

An hour or two later, stuffed with delicacies, guests rose to return to card games, gossip, and dancing. It was well past one, and though I felt a yawn tickling the back of my throat, others seemed prepared to continue until dawn.

The Darcys, the Bexleys, the Fitzwilliams, and Miss Vane were gathered and talking. Miss Darcy moved to make space for me in their circle. "Miss Bennet has been assisting at the foundling home, when I was not commanding her assistance with the ball, that is."

Marking my confusion, Mrs Fitzwilliam explained, "I was sharing that I shall be seeking ways to occupy my time in some useful way."

Miss Vane looked as if she had eaten bad fish. "Have you no estate?"

"We have only just returned," said Mrs Fitzwilliam. "And my husband has no inherited family lands to speak of."

"Second son," the colonel added cheerfully.

Miss Vane blinked slowly, as was her way. Was she pondering a lack of land or simply attempting to comprehend the words being spoken? Then her head swivelled to me. "Why do you devote time to foundlings?"

"They need assistance," I replied simply.

"Surely a donation would do," said Miss Vane.

"In addition to the fact that I have not the funds to give away..." Was I right to confess such a personal matter? I thought not, yet something in Miss Vane forced indelicate and combative words from me. "I prefer to be present. When one donates money, it allows for distance. I enjoy speaking to the workers and holding the infants."

She raised her eyebrows. "If you had children of your own, such a venture would not be necessary." The comment felt like a slap and I suspected she might have intended it as such.

"So I shall, when I find a man worth marrying." I felt the heat rise in my cheeks and was aware of my impertinence, but was unable to stop. "And even then, I hope not to be so consumed with myself that I cannot attend to those in need. There are many less fortunate, and while we go about in fine carriages and silk gowns, allowing others to tend to our every need, many people are suffering and starving and worse."

My words, delivered with unchecked fervour, were greeted by a silence that informed me of my error. Others' laughter drifted past us. My stomach hurt. Breath would not come. My incurable honesty would—

"I quite agree," said Mrs Fitzwilliam. "It was the reason I ran towards a war. I could not sit in a drawing room talking about it, I wished to be active in it."

"And thank heavens you did," said the colonel, kissing her hand, and she beamed.

Mr Alexander Bexley asked, "Now that you have returned, Colonel, where are you bound? Do you plan to remain in the military?"

"First, we shall visit with my family. Beyond that I am not certain."

As the conversation continued, I noted Mr Darcy stealing glances at me. Were they glances of disapproval, given my recent comments, or something of a more flattering sort?

I thought he might ask me to dance the last dance, but he did not, though a gentleman I had been introduced to some months ago did. It was a pleasant way to spend half an hour, though it held no promise of anything of significance.

Was Mr Darcy watching all of the dancers or was it just me? Did I, perhaps, stand a little straighter and ensure that my steps were just that much more delicate? Indeed. Was I proud of this? No. But it could not be helped.

CHAPTER 27

By the first light of dawn, the last of the guests had departed. Miss Vane had gone upstairs to her guest room hours earlier, but others lingered chatting amiably even after the musicians had packed up their instruments and exited through the kitchens.

My feet and back had ached, but I desired to see the ball through to the last. Miss Darcy, though her eyes drooped, smiled contentedly as the Bexleys bade us farewell at last, along with some distant Darcy cousins who had had so much to drink that two servants were required to lift them into their carriage. Mrs Fitzwilliam offered an elbow to help her husband up the stairs, a reversal that might have embarrassed some men, but which the colonel seemed to find endearing. "Ever my caretaker," he said, kissing her cheek as they ascended.

"Georgiana," Mr Darcy said, "it is time you went to bed."

She pouted. "Brother, once I lay my head down, this shall all be finished and in the past."

"Indeed," I said, noting that she swayed with fatigue. "It has come to an end, but the sooner you rest, the sooner we can discuss the event. We can pore over every minute detail as many times as you wish."

She smiled through heavy lids. "Do you promise?"

"Yes. I shall return at...let us say two o'clock, and we can begin."

"Return?" asked Mr Darcy.

"Yes," I said, noting the increasing dimness as servants snuffed out the last of the candles. "As planned, I shall reside with my aunt and uncle in Gracechurch Street for the duration of your stay. I only remained last night due to your delay."

Miss Darcy swayed and startled. "You are asleep on your feet!" I cried. "To bed."

She stumbled up the stairs to where Miss Mitchell would be waiting, perhaps dozing in a chair, to ready her for bed. Miss Darcy murmured, "So much planning and anticipation for one evening's festivities and now *poof*, it is finished."

"Poof, indeed," Mr Darcy murmured, watching her go, contentment smoothing his features. Then he turned to me and a small frown returned. "You could stay in your room upstairs as Georgiana's guest."

I shook my head. "The carriage awaits, and my aunt and uncle are expecting me."

I looked about at the now-empty rooms, their candles half-used, the chalk pictures smudged on the floor, glasses and teacups left on tables here and there, the white flowers shimmering in the dawn's gentle beams. I sighed. "It was a beautiful affair."

"Thanks to you."

I shook my head, but Mr Darcy stepped closer and repeated, in a low voice, "Thanks to you."

I should have backed away. Instead, I leant just a bit closer. Everything was still and quiet somehow. Where was the noise of the early morning city? Where were the servants with their tasks that rattled and clattered?

Not wanting to break the stillness but compelled to speak, I attempted to think of something beyond our bodies, so near that his breath ruffled the loose curls at my temples. I said quietly, "Miss Darcy deserves every happiness."

"You will never comprehend how dear it is to me that you are the one who brought her that happiness. After so many heartbreaks, our parents, Thomas—I feared I would lose her to unhappiness or…or disaster. Ruin."

"Miss Darcy is resilient. If anything, you are losing her to your *own* unhappiness."

There was a pause. He closed his eyes and admitted, "I have lost myself to it."

I wanted to reach out and wrap my arms around him. Yet I remained still. "It need not be this way."

"No," he said. His eyes opened and locked onto mine.

His fingertips brushed my arm, sending a chill through my body. Then he pressed a fingertip under my chin to tip it up and our lips touched. This was what I remembered: the feeling of being lost to him. Of the perfection of his kiss. Of wanting nothing more than for it to go on and on.

I stepped in, our warm bodies touching. Instead of pushing me away as I feared he might, he pulled me closer and kissed me more deeply. All of these years I had wanted only him. It was why I had refused other men, and why I preferred to be alone: none other than Mr Darcy would do. He was all I wanted. He was all I had wanted since the first moment of our acquaintance. I could feel the pounding of his heart, galloping in time with my own.

"Elizabeth, you intoxicate me." He leant down and kissed me again. "I want to kiss you forever."

A scream rent the perfection of our moment. Mr Darcy sprang away from me and my head turned quickly towards the source of the noise.

Miss Vane stood tall and elegant and perfectly still, her mouth frozen in a little 'O'. She was as beautiful as a painting, even in her moment of distress and disappointment. Oh, to think she had believed she had snared Mr Darcy, only to come upon this sight.

"This is nothing," he told her quickly, taking a step backwards.

Nothing? That kiss was not nothing. How could he say such a thing?

"How dare you humiliate me like this?" she shrieked and some part of me marvelled that she was capable of speaking so quickly, of having interest in something.

"Lavinia," Mr Darcy said, "let us—"

Her eyes glittered meanly as she said to him, "It is no wonder you are attracted to such a girl as *her*—low-born, practically a pauper—given *your* situation."

Her words struck him silent for a moment. What situation? I wondered.

His face darkened and his fists clenched. I had never

seen him as angry, save for when Mr Wickham attempted to steal away Georgiana.

"Lavinia, come with me," he said, appearing to struggle to maintain his composure.

Her pretty face contorted into a snarling smile that held no joy. "Men easily ensnare women beneath them, as you know." Her eyes met mine. "Beware, Miss Bennet, or you shall be the next victim of the Darcy charm."

She threw her head back in a sharp, angry laugh. He stepped towards her, but she spun and ran up the stairs. "Do not follow me, Mr Darcy!"

He froze mid-stride, one foot reaching for the next step yet hovering. It would have been amusing if all had not been so disconcerting.

There was the sound of a door slammed above followed by the sound of another door opened. Was she returning? Or had her shouting roused other guests? Miss Darcy? Would this argument ruin her otherwise perfect night?

I opened my mouth, wanting to say something, anything, but my shock was so complete I could not form the words. I wanted to understand what Miss Vane's cruel words had meant. I wanted to beg Mr Darcy to come to my side and kiss me again. I wanted to ask why he had denied the importance of our kiss and had not confessed that we were meant to be together. But perhaps he did not believe it.

Colonel Fitzwilliam clacked down the steps in his dressing gown and robe, his face pale in the early light. He stopped at the step above Mr Darcy, who was gripping the baluster, his shoulders slumped. "What, pray, has caused Miss Vane to slam doors and sob in her chamber?"

Mr Darcy looked up at his cousin. I wish I could have seen whether his face was as lined with anguish as my own.

Colonel Fitzwilliam's gaze darted to me; seeing my expression, he looked quickly back to Mr Darcy. "Darcy, a word." He moved past his cousin with as much haste as he could with his injury.

Mr Darcy turned as if in a dream, not looking my way, and followed the colonel into a receiving room. As the door was not completely closed, I could hear them muttering, and when the conversation grew more heated, I heard more.

"But what did she mean about your situation?"

"She knows the truth. You know what I mean."

"How would she know?"

Mr Darcy mumbled something I could not hear.

"You must be joking," the colonel said angrily.

"No, she asked me to confirm it," Mr Darcy said slowly. "It is for the best. I could not have her accept me if—"

"Accept you? She does not make you happy."

"Nothing makes me happy."

"You have money and influence. If *you* cannot alter your fortune, what hope is there for the rest of us?"

"*You* are not burdened by expectation."

"Darcy, whose expectations burden you? Who is left to judge you? Ghosts? For a man as intelligent as you, I marvel that this fact eludes you."

"I made a promise."

"To whom? Miss Vane?"

Silence.

I crept closer.

"Kissing Miss Bennet—again, I might add!—was as good a promise as anything. And that girl is the one for you. You are blind, and a bigger fool than I realised, if you give her up." Mr Darcy might have said something in reply that I could not hear, but his cousin continued, "And as for the other matter, men such as yourself need not be troubled by missteps and secrets. Lands and a title will protect you. If anyone discovered the truth, they might disapprove, but clucking tongues shall not harm you."

"That is untrue. My reputation would be in tatters."

"Reputation." The word was coated with disgust. "You ought to have thought of that before you confirmed the truth to the spiteful Miss Vane." He approached the door but stopped. "And if I see you with her again, I shall never forgive you."

The colonel banged out into the entry, nearly running into me. He paused, nodded, and hobbled up the stairs, the sound of his cane fading as he went.

I stood and waited, but Mr Darcy did not emerge. My heart hammered. What was I to do? Leave? Wait? I waited. I counted to one hundred, then to one hundred and fifty. He did not appear, nor did I hear another sound.

Sleep's talons were digging into me, and the day grew brighter by the moment. I could go to Mr Darcy as he could come to me. Yet neither of us did. Stubbornness or pride kept us rooted. I had said what I thought, shown how I felt. No, I would not beg for an answer and I would not beg for his kisses. He knew I was here. It was why, coward that he was, he remained in that sitting room. Rage's flames licked up my neck.

Shaking my head, I picked my way to the front door and went to the carriage awaiting me. As we clattered towards my aunt and uncle's house, my body throbbed, my mind reeled, and I wondered how I would face Mr Darcy again.

CHAPTER 28

At two o'clock, as promised, despite simultaneous feelings of excitement and dread, I knocked on the door of the Grosvenor Street house. The housekeeper escorted me to the drawing room where Miss Darcy awaited. Though purple had emerged under her eyes, she looked lovely and content, unlike myself; I was unsettled and furious, and likely more fatigued than she, for I did not sleep, tossing and turning all morning.

Rising from the sofa, she reached out her arms. "How wonderful that you came." We embraced, and when I sat, she poured tea. "I hope you will stay here again beginning tonight. My brother and Miss Vane departed this morning, so you might move back to your room if your aunt and uncle can continue to spare you."

"They departed? Why?"

She shrugged. "He would not say. As long as it is not to marry her, I shall be content. I was surprised, however, by their sudden departure. They were meant to stay for weeks more." She sipped delicately. "She did seem unhappy at the ball. Everyone else appeared to enjoy it. It *was* a pleasing affair, was it not?" She looked at me with wide eyes, clearly in need of reassurance.

In spite of my hammering heart, I forced a smile. "It was the finest ball I have ever attended. If she could not enjoy it, the problem lies within her."

A voice came from behind. "The problem lies within who?" The Fitzwilliams came into view.

"Miss Vane," said Miss Darcy.

The Fitzwilliams shifted uncomfortably. So, he had told his wife of last night's events, but Miss Darcy remained unaware. If only I had the luxury of not knowing what little I knew.

"Well," the colonel said, "they are gone. All we can do" —at this he looked hard at me— "is wait." He escorted his wife to a seat and a servant poured them tea.

I lifted the cup to my lips but did not drink for fear I could not keep it down. How was I to pretend all was well when I was in such a state?

Miss Darcy set down her cup. "Miss Bennet, a message was delivered. The day after tomorrow the Bexleys will escort us to the Royal Academy of Art! Is that not thrilling?"

I nodded, working my face into a mask of the expected expression. How was I to continue speaking of the Bexleys when my mind returned and returned to the kiss and Miss Vane and their disappearance and the argument, and... No, I had to push it all away. "What did you enjoy most about your ball, Miss Darcy?"

"I feared being the centre of attention, yet it was not

overly frightful. I enjoyed the music, the food, the company. Every plan we made was perfect."

On and on she spoke; the Fitzwilliams and I nodded in time. While I truly desired to know her thoughts, my mind drifted. It could not have been easy for Mr Darcy and Miss Vane to arrange travel so quickly. Did they take all of their possessions or would some be sent after? How long would he be gone? Why was there not even a note sent to the Gardiners? No, he could not have written directly to me, but to depart so was untenable.

Why could I not let him go? Yet he made the overture to me. He made me believe this was a possibility. No, it was more than that. As his cousin said, that kiss was as good as a promise.

Mrs Fitzwilliam chimed in, and once the two ladies were happily talking about the fashions of the guests, Colonel Fitzwilliam asked for a word. We strode to the window, looking out at the bustling road of carriages and vendors, servants, and nobles, all with business that each of them thought more important than anything in the world. What cared they for my disappointment and confusion?

The colonel ran his fingers through his hair, which had, I realised, grown lighter since first we met. I suspected it was due to exposure to the sun in France.

"My cousin is stubborn."

"Yes."

"He will not listen to reason."

I swallowed a lump in my throat. Did he mean 'reason' to be Mr Darcy's refusal to be with me? Was I once and for all overthrown?

The colonel said, "He promised he would write once things had been settled."

"*What* had been settled?"

"I cannot say." Our eyes locked, and he added, "Miss Bennet, I will beg for your discretion about last night." He frowned. "I know I cannot beg your patience, for he has tested it long enough, but let us not give up on our hopes."

"*Our*—"

"Dearest," Mrs Fitzwilliam called, "would you care for more tea?"

He lowered his pointed chin to his chest and breathed deeply. "A good wife," he said to her, "keeps one in tea and happiness." To me he intoned, "If only my cousin could see it."

Two days later, Miss Darcy and I were off to the Royal Academy of Art. My feet were still sore from the ball, though I pretended they were not, and I acted as if I was not thinking endlessly of Mr Darcy, which I was.

Miss Darcy and Mr William Bexley chatted amiably as they walked through an exhibit, pointing to canvases and sculptures along the way, while Mr Alexander Bexley and I strolled a few steps behind, trailed by our chaperon, Mrs Lewis, a distant cousin of the Darcys who escorted us when needed. Though Mrs Younge's name was never mentioned after the unfortunate incidents at Ramsgate, the lesson about trusting strangers had been learnt.

"What do you think of the painting?" Mr Bexley asked Miss Darcy.

"I... What do *you* think?"

"I quite like it."

"I do as well."

It was an insipid conversation, but I knew she was nervous about her first outing with a true suitor. The day prior, Miss Darcy had been called on by three different young men, and found this new attention both thrilling and terrifying.

"Miss Bennet," Mr Alexander Bexley asked, "do you enjoy art?"

"I do. And ballet and opera and theatre and musicales. I like all forms of entertainment."

He extended an arm and I took it, which improved our ability to stay in step, though not my attraction to him. What little I had felt at the ball dissipated the moment Mr Darcy had kissed me. Again. Even so, I would be polite and attempt to enjoy the outing.

"Which would you say is your favourite?"

"I cannot make such a choice," I replied. "It depends on my mood."

"Are you fickle, then?"

"Not in my friendships, but I suppose in other matters I am. I enjoy all foods, all art, all gowns, all dogs, and most places. I enjoy new experiences and meeting new people."

He laughed. "Why that is marvellous!"

He was handsome, to be sure, and kind. Thoughtful, as well. And yet there was no spark. Even Mr Corbet, the last proposal I had refused, had made my heart race when he was near. But perhaps racing hearts and wild imaginings were not necessary for a happy life. I could not imagine my parents swooning for one another, though were they truly happy? I believed they might be. And upon reflection, I recalled each of them telling me of joyous early days and their excitement at their wedding and in the days and years that followed. Mr Bexley elicited no thrill, but was that necessary? Respect and peace could do. But what of stimulation of the mind and spirit? What of the swirl of passion I felt for Mr Darcy? Was that necessary? Did I ask too much of a marriage?

Mary had told me, 'Marry a decent man. He need not be the most handsome, the most exciting or have the most money. He simply needs to suit you well enough.' Could Mr Alexander Bexley be the gentleman to suit me well enough? It was possible.

But when we entered the Grosvenor Street house, having said our goodbyes to the gentlemen, Colonel Fitzwilliam waved me into the library, leaving his wife to ask Miss Darcy about the outing.

"I have had a letter, the subject of which you might take interest."

I held my breath. Dare I hope or ought I to fear his next words?

"Miss Vane," he said, "has gone on to Scotland. Without Darcy."

Without Mr Darcy. She went on alone. They were not together. Whatever had occurred? I blinked at him, unable to form questions, and unsure if I should.

"He wrote that he is bound for Pemberley. He hired an escort so that Miss Vane could have her carriage take her on to Scotland. He says he will return to town when he is able." He looked at me expectantly, but what was I to say? Mr Darcy had not emerged from the sitting room to speak to me and had departed London without saying goodbye. The man was impossible! Something was damaged within him, and it would be best for me to find someone undamaged by whatever it was that troubled Mr Darcy so.

"I hope," I said, then cleared my throat, attempting to find my voice. "I hope he enjoys the peace of the country."

"Is that all?" Colonel Fitzwilliam crossed his arms tight against his chest. "I had suspected you might have more of a tender interest in the matter."

I pressed my lips together but admitted nothing.

He ran his fingers through his hair, pulling at the ends in exasperation. "I told my wife this would be the case. You both are doing all you can to ruin your lives."

"I have given him every opportunity to begin again what we started before his brother died, and for years, I prayed merely for him to be civil! He is—"

"A fool. But do not let his behaviour fool you. He has loved you since the moment he saw you at Longbourn."

I shook my head. "If he truly loved me, he would not have cast me aside as he did."

"His parents were formidable. Forbidding."

I felt tears pricking at my eyes. "No, Colonel. Mr Bexley has been...very attentive to me, and if my future lies not with him, someone else could—"

I did not mean it. I wanted Mr Darcy. I wanted him with all my heart. But if I allowed myself to admit it, the pain would be too much. Mr Darcy had walked away from me again and again, and I could not allow him to control my feelings thus.

I walked out of the library and to the front door, pulling it open.

"Miss Bennet," he called out, "where are you going?"

"I must be away from here."

"What shall I tell Miss Darcy?"

Miss Darcy, my sweet, sweet friend did not deserve to be abandoned by me as so many had abandoned her for her entire life. "Please tell her I am weary from our excursion and shall return tomorrow morning."

I curtseyed, though avoided meeting his gaze, and departed.

CHAPTER 29

When I arrived at Gracechurch Street, a letter in Jane's hand was offered to me.

Dearest Lizzy,

I hope you will soon come to us at Netherfield. I have been without you nearly half a year and I wish to be with you before my confinement begins, for I know all shall be altered once a child arrives. I desire to walk with you as we once did, and to confide in and laugh with each other. Although Charles is full of nervous joy, I fear the loneliness of confinement, and, in truth, I always dreamt of bringing new life into the world with you at my side. Now that the time is approaching, I cannot help but fear what awaits, but I know that I shall feel more at ease if we face this together.

Your loving sister,
Jane

My beloved sister was correct: all would change once she was a mother, and we had spent too much time apart these past few years. More importantly, she needed me. She mentioned fear, and I could not consider losing another sister. I would go as soon as I could arrange things.

But how long before I could extricate myself from London? I thought a fortnight would do. Unlike Mr Darcy, I would not run from Miss Darcy, but I did need time to sort out whether I would live at Netherfield or Longbourn, and bid those at the Foundling Hospital a proper farewell.

The next day, I returned to Grosvenor Street with the intention of remaining there until my departure. Miss Darcy was on a walk with the Fitzwilliams, so I made my way upstairs.

I opened the door to my room and stopped short. Georgiana's lady's maid was sitting on the tufted chair at my dressing table weeping.

"Miss Mitchell?" I asked.

She leapt up, swiping at her face. Keeping her gaze low, she bobbed a curtsey, begged my pardon, and hurried to the door, hoping, I assume, to make a quick escape. However, I did not step aside. Her swollen eyes, filled with pleading, met mine. I knew she desired to depart, but how could I allow one in such distress to face her troubles alone?

"What ails you?"

She pressed her lips together as if willing her tale to remain a secret.

I touched her shoulder. I had meant it as a kindly gesture, but she flinched, so I pulled back. "You may tell me. What is troubling you?"

She shook her head, her cheeks even redder than before.

"You know I am not the mistress of the house. I have no power here."

Gaze fixed to the ground, she said, "You are friends with Miss Darcy and Mr Darcy. I cannot."

"I shall not betray your confidence. I have no desire to hurt you and might even be able to help."

A loud sob escaped her lips and she covered her face with her hands. I sprang into action, shutting the door to block the sound of her cries from the hall and leading her to the window-seat. She perched there carefully, her face red with as much mortification as anguish. I sat in a chair and began my enquiries.

"Did someone," I began, making my voice as gentle as I could manage, "hurt you? Another servant or—" I hesitated, hoping Mr Darcy was not this sort of man "—a gentleman?"

She shook her head and I breathed out relief.

"Did Mrs Harris scold you?"

Another shake of the head.

"Then what? Are you in love?"

At this, the sobs grew loud again. Though she was clearly upset, I was relieved, for I could much more manage a girl thwarted in love better than one having been attacked by a man.

"Have you told him of your feelings?"

"I told him, and he vanished."

"Then he is not worth your worry. You shall find another."

"But I need *him*."

"No girl needs a particular boy. Especially one who prefers to run away. There are other—"

"He is the father." She rested her hands on her belly.

Realisation struck me and I closed my eyes a moment. Not attacked, and yet such a consequence...

What was she to do? Unmarried. No family to speak of. The servants in this house and neighbourhood had been a substitute family for her, and they loved her dearly. Yet there was nothing any of them might do to assist her in her condition. Their salaries were too paltry to support a fellow servant plus a child, and they could not secret her away in spare rooms. She would be let go the moment she began showing and her secret was out, and then what? She was well and truly in a bind. Girls such as she were referenced as a caution and never spoken of in any detail that might allow me to reassure her.

"Who else knows?"

"Only the father."

"Who is he?"

Her eyes grew wide. "I daren't say! He would be angry."

My worry for the girl only increased. "And you say he vanished?"

"Left town after Miss Darcy's ball. Wouldn't say when he might return, but not to tell anyone of our secret."

Our secret. Left town.

My breath stopped. Could it be— Could the father be Mr Darcy? It was unthinkable, and yet Miss Vane had known of a secret. What had she said? 'Men easily ensnare women beneath them', and 'Beware, Miss Bennet, or you shall be the next victim of the Darcy charm'.

Miss Mitchell was of a rank beneath him and in his employ, and as easily as I had fallen victim to the Darcy charm, she might have, as well. How easy it was for a man to hide his misdeeds, leaving women to face the consequences. Miss Vane and I suffered broken hearts, while Miss Mitchell... How could he leave her so alone?

How could I love a man who had done such a thing? Miss Mitchell would be dismissed without character and have no means of taking care of her child. It was unfair. A father could simply run away from his responsibility while a mother was left, literally and metaphorically, to carry the burden. It was a repellent fact of life. If this was true, if Mr Darcy was capable of such a thing, he could never be for me. Not after this.

"I do not know what can be done but I promise you that I will do all that I can to ensure your care."

Truly, I did not know what I could do, and I soon grew busy. Over the following few weeks, I supervised the packing of my belongings, and said my goodbyes to acquaintances and friends, including Mrs Lambert and her family. Mrs Lambert's baby was growing fast, and I feared how different she would be when next I saw her. I nuzzled my nose against little Abigail's neck, loving the softness of her skin, wondering whether I would ever have a child of my own.

Mrs Lambert and I promised to write. Mrs Festing hugged and hugged me, saying I always had a home with her if needed before whispering against my ear that she was sure Mr Darcy would come to his senses, but that if he hurt me again, she would put him over her knee and spank him as she still did with her youngest. Despite my despair over what he had done, and my decision to never accept him even if he offered, imagining this spanking set us both to giggling so much we forgot our tears and left in laughter, as only seemed right.

Miss Darcy, however, was inconsolable as I made to leave Grosvenor Street. I reached for her hand and lifted it, kissing her knuckles. "I shall return. Our friendship is not at an end. Merely a pause in our companionship as I serve another sister in need."

When Miss Darcy turned into Mrs Fitzwilliam's shoulder, the older woman said, "Colonel Fitzwilliam has already written to Mr Bingley, and we shall come to Netherfield once the baby is a month old." Miss Darcy lifted her head and looked at Mrs Fitzwilliam, who dried the girl's tears with her thumbs. "It shall not be a long absence, darling. We shall all be together again soon."

"I cannot bear being apart!"

"Dear Miss Darcy," I said, "Mr Bexley is an attentive suitor, but not so attentive that he would stay at the inn in Meryton to woo you." At this, she smiled, and I pressed her hand. She was young, and appeared especially so in this moment, so I felt compelled to offer one last bit of advice. "Look to like him, but be certain he is the right match before accepting any offers, his or that of whoever else might come along. You are yet full young, there is a great deal out there for you to experience and learn."

"How will I know without you to guide me?"

Colonel Fitzwilliam stepped forward. "As one of your guardians, I declare there shall be no immediate weddings, so Miss Bennet is safe to leave us for a little while." When Miss Darcy pouted, he pinched her cheeks and said, "How can we miss her if she never leaves?"

Mrs Fitzwilliam came forwards for a last embrace, the colonel bowed, and I entered the carriage. I had thought to take the stage, but my hosts would not hear of it and sent me in one of Mr Darcy's many conveyances.

———

"Welcome home, Lizzy!" My father's outstretched arms enfolded me when I stepped down from the carriage onto Longbourn's drive a few hours later.

I turned to my mother, and kissed both of her cheeks. Even in the bright sun, I could see she was pale. Had grief for Mary taken such a toll on her? Perhaps. Or perhaps nerves had overwhelmed her of late, as concern for Jane likely was weighing on her.

"Dear Lizzy," she said. "It is so good to have you home, though I had hoped when next we saw you, it would be with news of a husband!"

I attempted a smile. My parents and I walked into the house, where tea awaited us. My father took the chair across from mine. "It is quiet with only Lydia and Kitty at Longbourn. We know you will likely stay with Jane for her confinement, but that is a ways off, so I hope you will remain with us until that is near."

I nodded. It was what I had planned, but now that I was at Longbourn, I feared the emptiness left behind by Mary threatened to overwhelm me. How strange. For most of the years that I lived here with her, I gave her little thought, and when I did, I was pained to recall, it mostly was uncharitable. But after our days in Ramsgate, my fondness for her had grown; now, back in the home we had shared, she filled my thoughts. I had to hope that time would ease these feelings.

Mama asked, "Did all go as planned for Miss Darcy at the ball?"

"Yes. She was very pleased. As was I."

"And did *she* find a husband?"

I laughed. "It has been but two weeks, and she is not quite seventeen, after all. I do not think Mr Darcy would allow her to marry until she is at least eighteen, but I will say one prospect looks promising. He is kind and—"

"What is his income?"

"Hush, now," my father interrupted. "The Darcys have no need for such enquiries, and it is not polite to ask."

"I cannot ask my own daughter?" She crossed her arms and pouted. "If we had had the funds to hold balls, perhaps all of our girls would be married by now."

"Mama, balls would not have brought me someone I liked well enough, and the expense would have been too great." I squeezed my mother's hand. "I wish to see Jane—who married without the expense of a ball." I gave my father a sly look. He looked pleased and winked in reply.

My mother was less so. "Go to visit Jane already? You have only just arrived!" she protested.

"Yes, and the ride was arduous. I am in need of a walk."

"Why not eat a proper meal first?" Papa asked. "Hill arranged for your favourites."

The pleading in his eyes was not just so Cook's work

would not go untasted and unappreciated. I would battle back my desire to flee, to run until my lungs hurt. I would see to my belongings and eat the delicacies offered. I would chat and pretend that I was not screaming within to escape.

CHAPTER 30

Later that afternoon, I arrived at Netherfield Park. Jane was still moving about freely, so I was escorted to her in the drawing room. She looked plump and serene, though she made a fuss about being hideous. We talked and talked as if months had not passed, and when the sun began to set, she begged me not to depart.

"Mama and Papa are expecting me at Longbourn tonight, but I shall return here for good in two days and remain with you here until the babe arrives. It was a disappointment to them that I came to you today."

She squeezed my hand. "I know it pains you to be at that house, but it was our home for so long. Embrace the memories. There were many good ones, dearest. Many, many good ones."

On my walk back to Longbourn, I thought on her advice. Yes, there had been many good memories. A lifetime of them. The births of my sisters, learning to play the pianoforte and laughing at my many errors, picking flowers for bouquets in our garden, dance lessons led by

Mama, outings to Meryton, watching one pig give birth to the largest litter of piglets ever recorded in the region and little Lydia taking the runt and attempting to put doll dresses on it but settling for a tiny pelisse Jane made of fabric scraps. Every corner held echoes of joy and frustration, but it was my home and always would be, even when Mr Collins became its master. I entered the front door smiling, thinking of the reasons to be thankful.

The next day I spent indulging my sisters by walking with them into Meryton and waiting as they touched every ribbon and piece of lace. I bought each girl one of their choosing. Upon our return, I wrote letters to Mrs Lambert, Charlotte, and Miss Darcy, then sat in the garden reading for a time, remembering Mary smelling the roses each summer, and forcing myself to look at the memory fondly rather than as a source of pain. Meals were lively, which was a delightful change from the quiet companionability of those at Grosvenor Street. Indeed, I made a concerted effort to forget all about those at that house, one gentleman in particular.

Most of my belongings had already been brought to Netherfield, so there was nothing to pack. That evening I slid into the bed I once shared with Jane and now with Kitty. Kitty had complained that I ought to stay in Mary's room, but when I suggested she might do the same, she clapped her lips shut, took a moment, and said she welcomed the two nights with me as her bedfellow. Neither of us believed in ghosts, but we did not like that room anymore, despite its lovely window seat overlooking the garden.

The next months were delightful. Jane and I walked,

did needlework, read books, spoke of our futures and the past, which made us laugh, and occasionally cry. Bingley and I grew better acquainted, which was a gift, for he was a gentle, generous soul, and I came to appreciate even more how perfect he was for my Jane.

Every Sunday, after services, I returned to Longbourn with my family for dinner; occasionally I spent the night. Mama shared plans for her garden, and Papa showed me new books he had procured for his library. My younger sisters asked me to help them practise their dances and to teach them new card games. I was prone to bouts of melancholy and could be impatient, but endeavoured not to allow myself to be vexed. They meant well, and we all loved each other in spite of our foibles.

One hot August afternoon when I returned to Netherfield from an overnight visit to Longbourn, I was surprised to see the servants racing frantically about. A footman told me it was about Jane and the baby, but could not say more, so I ran up the stairs to her room, fearful the news was bad, but found her peacefully sitting.

She turned to me and said, "Heavens, Lizzy, you look as if you'd seen a ghost!"

"I feared you had become one, the way the servants were carrying on."

"I had a twinge this morning and it set off a flutter."

I sat beside her, looking at her placid face and perfectly tied dressing gown. "A twinge?"

"More than a twinge, I suppose. Several twinges. Regular twinges." She winced just as she finished speaking.

"Another twinge?" I asked evenly.

A nod as she blew out the breath she had been holding. "The babe seems to wish to arrive sooner than expected."

Indeed, at least a few weeks early. Jane's ungainly girth and recent discomfort made sense now. "You need not pretend bravery," I said tenderly.

"It is not pretending to be brave, Lizzy," she groaned. "I am attempting to conserve energy. I understand first births can be lengthy."

Neither of us mentioned that a first birth could be deadly, as well. "What can I do to help the time pass?"

"Hold my hand. And do not leave my side."

I kissed her temple and made good on my promise.

The following afternoon, Edmund was born to an exhausted, relieved, and joyful Jane, and to Bingley, whose state matched that of his beloved wife. I left them to their felicitations and napped for a while.

When I emerged once again from my chamber, refreshed and anxious to see my nephew, I heard the laughter of my family coming from below. I did not believe Jane would be out of bed so soon, and went to her room first.

Servants tiptoed about as she slept, so I eased myself out and descended the stairs. My sisters sat in a corner of the receiving room giggling and gossiping while my parents questioned Bingley about every conceivable detail of the birth that he knew of, which was scant. Jane had insisted all be far from her cries and moans, save her maid, me, and a midwife (another insistence, though a doctor sat at the ready below). Jane had performed bravely, but the entire business had been far more terrifying than I had imagined and made me think I preferred being an aunt to a mother, at least for the time being.

I picked up a glass to participate in the toast, smiling at Bingley with pure joy. He was a good match for Jane, and she had survived this ordeal. More than survived; she had comported herself beautifully.

"The child is well, as is Jane," said Bingley. "That is all that matters to me."

"Indeed," said my father, clapping him on the shoulder. They sat and, though I was meant to sit with the family, I excused myself. I was in need of a walk.

I put on my boots and a more sensible gown, and slipped out the front door. As I moved towards the path that eventually snaked into a stand of trees—the only wild part of Netherfield's otherwise manicured lands—I heard a rider approaching the house. Curious as ever, I stood in the shadows to see who it might be.

It was Mr Darcy.

Could he have received news of the birth so soon? Not if he had been at Pemberley, or even in town. No, he must have been coming here independently. Beholding him, I reminded myself that I did not know whether the situation with Miss Mitchell was anything to do with him. Suspicious as it was, there might be a good explanation and I only hoped I might learn what it was, even if I half feared confirmation of the worst.

I walked back towards the front door and arrived as he dismounted, servants ready to take his horse. And what was the meaning of his being on a horse rather than in one of his fine carriages?

As he smoothed his coat, he spotted me.

"Mr Darcy, I did not expect to see you here."

"I— Why— Oh, your sister. Has she—"

"Jane has given Bingley a son, and both are healthy. It was only this afternoon, so my family is within."

"Just this afternoon?" He removed his hat and ran one hand through his hair. "My timing could not be more disastrous."

I laughed, which pulled him up short. "I was going to say your timing could not be better, but we seem to have different views."

He grimaced and it was then that I noted his sunken cheeks and pale complexion, and the way his clothing fairly hung from his lean frame.

"Are you unwell, sir?"

"No, I am well. I should leave."

"Do not be foolish. You must enter and wish your friend well and see his baby."

"I must not *do* anything, Miss Bennet." He grimaced. "I apologise. I am hungry and tired, and—"

"All the more reason to enter. Take a moment for rest and sustenance. And then you might disappear again as you please." I regretted my pointed final words, but he did not react. Then my thoughts turned to Miss Mitchell, and my anger flared. "How fortunate for men that they have the freedom to disappear, even when they have responsibilities they ought to undertake."

He waved off the perplexed groom and frowned. "I am sorry I departed London so hastily. It was imperative that Miss Vane understand—"

"I do not speak of Miss Vane."

He tugged at his waistcoat. "Yes, I ought to have spoken to you the evening of the ball."

"I do not speak of myself either, though, yes, you ought to have."

His brow lowered. "I am tired, Miss Bennet, and I do not appreciate guessing games. Whatever are you troubled by?"

"Miss Mitchell."

He stared at me blankly.

Working to keep my voice at an acceptably low volume, I said, "Your sister's maid. You abandoned her."

"Abandoned her? *What?*"

"Can you honestly tell me you have no idea what I refer to?"

"Yes, I can. Pray, Miss Bennet, stop speaking in riddles and tell me directly what you mean."

It was far more difficult to utter the words than I imagined. His fierce expression did nothing to put me at ease. "She is with child." When he did not react, I said, "*Your* child."

"And this is what you think of me?" He stared at me, disbelief on every feature. "You think I would be foolish enough—nay, immoral enough—to take advantage of a maid? How poorly you think of me."

"I overheard you and your cousin— He spoke of secrets and missteps, and reputations in tatters."

He levelled his gaze at me. "You were eavesdropping?"

"You left me in the hall and I have good hearing."

"And you assumed *that*?" He tugged at his chin. "How disappointing to know you think so little of me."

I studied my shoes, willing my cheeks to cease their

burning. "You left, and Miss Vane said I might be another woman to fall victim to the Darcy charm."

His barking laugh pulled me up short. "Darcy charm? I do not know whether she was being ironic, but she is cruel, and alluded to something else entirely. To matters she was not at liberty to share. We parted ways because of her indiscretion. I could never attach myself to a woman who was deliberately cruel."

It was more information than I could comprehend. Each word he uttered prompted more questions.

He studied me a moment. "Speaking of tender hearts, you seem quite concerned with my servant. Would you explain Miss Mitchell's predicament?"

"She is in a family way, caused by a gentleman who, learning of her condition, departed town the day after Miss Darcy's ball."

Comprehension spread across his face. "The same day I left."

"That is all she said, other than being terrified. I offered help—"

His expression softened. "Of course you did."

"But I know not what I might do. She is in your employ, and you would be within your rights to dismiss her without a reference. But Mr Darcy, consider the terrible fate that might befall her and the child."

He looked to the sky, which was growing increasingly dark with clouds. "I shall think on it." Then he walked up the stairs where two footmen stood waiting to open the door.

In the parlour, he was greeted with amazement by Bingley and displeasure by Mama. I wished she might forget the slights of the past, but she was not inclined towards forgiveness and I feared he had slighted her and her girls too many times. Even so, he had given me purpose and a way out of my misery by asking me to spend time with Miss Darcy and I wished she would remember that.

Mr Darcy congratulated Bingley, and the men toasted, but then Bingley must have seen what I had observed before: Mr Darcy's fatigue and his sickly countenance. Bingley quickly took him to another room.

I decided to visit Jane. In truth, I also hoped to see or hear Mr Darcy, but Netherfield had enough rooms and thick enough doors that that proved impossible.

Jane was awake with Edmund in her arms. The baby fussed, but as Jane cooed to him, he settled. A wet nurse had been secured and sat in a room nearby. At least Edmund would be ensconced in this house, unlike some babes who were sent away until the weaning was completed some eighteen months later. Surely some mothers visited their progeny daily, but many did not, preferring nursemaids and nannies to bring their children to them for little more than the occasional inspection. Had the Darcys been such a family? I suspected his parents were aloof, or visited only to belittle and frighten their children.

No, I realised with a start. That could not be so. Miss Darcy spoke of contentment. However, both she and Mr Darcy indicated that he had been treated differently from his brother and sister. Why?

Jane's voice broke into my thoughts. "Is he not the most beautiful babe that ever lived?"

"Naturally," I said, sitting on the edge of her bed. "Climb in."

"I dare not."

"Why? Mama cannot make a scene over it, for she is forbidden from entering this chamber until tomorrow."

I offered an exaggerated gasp. "Sister, you have given a command?"

She lifted her chin. "As a mother myself, I have the prerogative to do so."

I snuggled against her. "Quite right."

Edmund's eyes darted behind closed lids and his little lips twitched into a semblance of a smile that made us chuckle.

Bingley knocked and entered. "My darling—Oh, Lizzy." I began to extricate myself from the bed, but he said, "Stay. I simply wanted to say that Mr Darcy would be spending the night at Netherfield. He will remain in his room and depart at daybreak, so you will not be bothered."

"It is no bother to me," Jane said, "as long as he does not enter *this* room. Why the hasty decampment?"

Bingley's eyes darted to me then back to his wife. "He did not expect us to have had the babe, nor to have company. He sends his apologies for not having sent word in advance." He bowed and left us alone.

"Whatever could that have been about?" she asked.

I stroked Edmund's cheek lightly, eliciting another twitch of a smile. "Who knows when it comes to Mr Darcy?"

He would be in his rooms, giving me no opportunity to

apologise for my assumptions or to enquire after Miss Mitchell's future. It was, perhaps, best this way.

"Lizzy, I have another matter to enquire about. Would you be Edmund's godmother?"

I sat up quickly, jostling mother and child enough that I had to beg pardon for their distress. Then I said, "Of course! An honour, Jane. Thank you!"

CHAPTER 31

In October, after six weeks of anticipation, the day of the christening dawned bright. The Fitzwilliams and the Darcys had come to Netherfield a week prior. Upon their arrival, I noted that Mr Darcy looked better than when I had last seen him, but did not yet seem fully restored. He kept to himself more than not, and was quiet at the table. I let him be, instead turning my attention to Miss Darcy and my sisters, and even Miss Mitchell, who had been brought along, though no mention of her situation or future had been made. Although I could see a new softness in the maid, she was, indeed, carrying quite small. I was not certain Miss Darcy was aware of her maid's predicament.

At the altar, Mr Darcy and I stood together, ready to be godparents. I desired to ask how he felt about this responsibility, wondering whether he took the religious aspect of it in earnest or if he saw himself as being more of an advisor to a young man coming of age. Mr Darcy had played a vital part in raising Miss Darcy, and she was one of the most delightful young women I knew. Having met Mr Bingley's sisters and brother-in-law, who were mercifully not in attendance, I thought his choice of Mr Darcy wise. Yes, he was a sensible choice, unless one's choice was to fall in love with him.

I struggled to turn my thoughts away from the man standing beside me, but I could feel his presence and smell his cologne. I could remember his embrace.

Jane looked healthier than ever, and beamed at Bingley. A week earlier when Jane was churched, our thanks had been given that both she and Edmund had escaped the infections that often took new mothers and babies. In this moment, I whispered my thanks once again for their health. Edmund seemed hearty, but these things were impossible to predict. I feared what could happen to Jane's delicate spirit if her child was taken from her. I stole a glance at my mother, who had lost her Mary. Mama had had one stillbirth and two miscarriages, but what woman saw all of her children live past infancy let alone childhood?

After the ceremony concluded, we all returned to Netherfield for a celebration where the drinks flowed more than was usual. Whether it was from relief over the health of Edmund and Jane or the discomfort of bringing the Darcys, Bennets, and Bingleys together, I could not say, but all were growing careless and less steady with each glass.

Mama remarked more than once on the loss of Mary and my 'determinedly' unmarried state. The colonel despaired about his leg and the physician who promised it would heal. Kitty and Lydia flirted with a new footman before being scolded by Jane.

Suddenly Mr Darcy's voice rose above the others. "As this is an evening of celebration, I would like all to know that Colonel and Mrs Fitzwilliam will be overseeing Pemberley for the near future. I shall depart soon for travel abroad."

"Travel?" I asked. "To where?"

He turned and looked at me. "That has yet to be determined. There is much of the world I wish to see, something I intended in my youth, but my plans were thwarted by the war and then the death of— Well, events prevented it."

"I remember," I murmured.

Mr Darcy had been so free, telling of his adventures with his cousin, eating new foods, seeing new lands. He had seemed alive.

"And will I—" said Miss Darcy, her lip quivering. "Will I be expected to remain at Pemberley with them?"

Mr Darcy gave her a small smile and shook his head. "No, you must be in town. I see that now. Perhaps Miss Bennet will accompany you?"

My mother sat up straight. "My daughter is not someone in your employ, Mr Darcy, that you are entitled to order about."

"Mama—" I said, but Mr Darcy was already apologising.

"Madam, pray, forgive me. I only meant if it was agreeable to her."

My mother lifted her chin and sat back in victory while my cheeks burnt. I wished he would have waited to announce this until after my family had departed, or asked me with fewer people about. What did I wish to do? Town was appealing but so was baby Edmund, and I had missed Jane so. Could I abandon my family indefinitely? Of course, had I already married, I would have left them.

"Mrs Bennet," said Papa, "it is late and time to depart."

Though she protested, she gathered my sisters and they left, the silence flooding the room noticeably. It was both a relief and an embarrassment.

"The day has been long," declared Miss Darcy, rising. "I shall bid you all good night."

"I quite agree," said Jane, and she rose, followed by Bingley, and expressed her well wishes and thanks for our making the day a joyous occasion.

Once the door was shut, Mrs Fitzwilliam turned to Mr Darcy. "It is beginning to be impossible to deny Miss Mitchell's condition. Your sister is innocent and does not recognise it, but it is not proper."

Colonel Fitzwilliam was swaying from drink. "Let the girl travel with us and have the child at Pemberley. She could even stay on as a maid."

"I cannot have her at Pemberley" Mr Darcy said. "Too many would believe the worst of me for that."

The hidden censure in his voice made my face burn but did not stop me from speaking. "Perhaps on a nearby farm?"

"None would take her," he said. "The shame is too much. We cannot."

Disappointed as I was, I understood that Mr Darcy was correct. I rose to excuse myself. I had just stepped out the door when I heard the colonel speak.

"Who would even know? No one visits Pemberley except for strangers who tour its magnificence when you are absent."

"It takes only one person to connect a gentleman with a maid and her bastard child. Believe me."

"If you do not help her—"

"Why should I do that? Why would I help a woman of low morals?"

"To judge Miss Mitchell given *your* past is ironic, Darcy."

There was a pause and then the sound of footsteps, moving fast. I immediately darted into the nearest empty room and heard him go past. I could only imagine the thunder that must have been on his brow.

Moments later, I heard the Fitzwilliams in the hall. "Ought I to go find him?" the colonel asked.

"It is late, and you have said rather enough. Speak to him tomorrow. It is well past time we ought to go to bed," his wife replied. I heard them begin their climb up the stairs.

I had to find Mr Darcy. Might he have stormed out to find solace in the woods? It was dark, but I would venture out if need be. He could not be left to his own misery.

I wandered down the hall, stopping first at Bingley's study. There was no answer to my knock. I looked into the music room, but it was empty. In the doorway of the library, I heard a stirring and entered, though it took a moment for my eyes to adjust to the near darkness.

Mr Darcy was sitting at a table covered with maps, holding his head in his hands.

CHAPTER 32

"Mr Darcy?"

He was out of his chair in a trice, and rushed towards me. The shock of his movement caused me to stumble back. It seemed he wished to slam the door upon me. "You should leave," he said.

I closed the door behind me and looked up at his anguished face. "Please tell me what troubles you."

"I cannot."

I remained still, my eyes misting at the pain in his voice.

"Can you not understand that your presence is not wanted? This is not a matter of any concern to you."

"Is it not?" He made no reply, so I pressed on. "I cannot leave another suffering, even when I know they desire solace."

"If you must meddle, go to one of your sisters."

"They do not need me."

"*I* do not need you."

"Yes, you do."

There was silence while I watched him stare at the floor.

"Please?" I swallowed hard. "I cannot bear to see you in agony. It pains me."

"Why?"

The only sound was our breath, rattling and quick.

"Because...because I care for you."

He raised his head and his eyes searched my face. "Why? Why would you care for me? As you know, I am temperamental, difficult—"

"And kind."

"I am not."

"I have *seen* it." I stepped closer, and, happily, he did not back away. "And loving. And intelligent and witty." He shook his head and I stepped closer still. "Please, you are my friend. Tell me what troubles you."

We stood in the dim room, brightened only by a single candle he must have lit earlier, yet it was enough to see his features twitch.

"I cannot understand it," he said in a low voice. "From the moment we met, I have desired to bare my soul to you."

I smiled a little, recalling our conversations in the woods.

He gestured for me to sit, and so I did. He perched on the edge of a neighbouring chair. "I am sorry that my cousin's words brought you into our family secrets."

"Sir, I am not certain what I heard. Only that you were upset by it."

He could evade the truth if he so desired. It would frustrate me not to know, but it might be better.

"What he spoke of is a secret that was not meant to be shared." Mr Darcy rose and strode to the window, turning his back to me. "He referred to my father."

"Your father? Is Miss—?" I stopped myself, mortified at my assumption.

"We are all his—Georgiana, Thomas, and I." He walked to the hearth and knelt, beginning a fire with logs and kindling prepared by the servants who discreetly smoothed the edges of life in this perfect abode. The flames leapt up and warmed his face. "I am my father's son, but not my mother's. Or rather, not Lady Anne Darcy's child. My mother was a maid at Pemberley."

Stunned, I sucked in a breath. "How did you learn of this?"

"After my parents died, I went through my father's study at Pemberley, organising and discarding items as needed. His private papers were hidden in a box that not even our housekeeper, Mrs Reynolds, knew of." His eyes drifted to the fire. "I found a note that was, apparently, tucked in with my blanket or basket or whatever I was abandoned with at Pemberley's doorstep. Why he would not have burnt the letter, I could not say."

"Perhaps it was the only piece of your mother that he had."

He sniffed an angry laugh. "*I* am the most significant piece left of her." He rose and strode to a mauve overstuffed chair facing the fire; he turned to me and gestured to the matching one. Once I sat, he lowered himself into his, his face lined with consternation. "In the letter, my mother—the woman who gave birth to me—said she knew she could not remain at the house in her condition and could not care for a babe without work, and that her dismissal once the housekeeper found out had assured that she would never again work in service."

"Do you think your father... Did he take advantage of her?"

He shook his head sharply. "She signed it 'love'. I believe—" He cleared his throat. "I believe there was some mutual affection there."

"Or entrapment."

"That would be possible, yet he kept the letter, which indicates he had feelings for her."

The clock ticked away.

"What happened to her?"

"Um..." He cleared his throat. "Mrs Reynolds heard that she killed herself after leaving me at Pemberley. And since all I have is this letter, I cannot know whether she suffered from melancholy and might have ended her life regardless, or if it was my birth that left her hopeless."

"Did none of the neighbours or their friends suspect that Lady Anne had not been with child?"

"She had been increasing. The child was lost just before I was brought to their door." He sighed heavily. "Mrs Reynolds said she had miscarried at least eight times between giving birth to Thomas and Georgiana."

"*Eight?*"

He nodded. "It was likely more."

"Poor lady." His eyes flew wide, but I added, "No one deserves that form of torment."

"True." His brow drew down.

"When I was left on Pemberley's doorstep, my parents retreated with me and with Thomas to Scotland and decided, it seems, to pass me off as their own. The distance and time away would allow for the appearance that the story was true. She must have confided in Lady Vane, which is how Miss Vane knew."

"Forgive my asking, but how could Lady Anne have allowed you to receive the family name?"

"My mother wanted another child and saw it as her opportunity to secure the Darcy line."

"But she also allowed for you to have *her* family name as your Christian name!"

He ran his hands along his gaunt cheeks. "Perhaps she was willing it to be true. It made the ruse more plausible."

"I cannot understand it."

"Nor I, if I am honest."

"So they placed you in line for inheritance."

"When Georgiana was, at last, born, there was great relief and joy, for they had another child of their own, but as she was a girl, it did not solve the problem of me or the line of succession. However, as long as Thomas remained healthy..."

He rose and strolled to the window again, looking out at the darkness. I could hear the distant chatter of servants somewhere in the hall. He stood in silence and I feared our conversation had concluded and that he had neglected to tell me. Then, still staring out the window, he spoke. "Often I asked myself why was my mother so especially disapproving of me." He turned, and I saw pain etched across his face. "For many years I blamed myself. I never was like the other Darcys." He leant the back of his head against the window and fixed his eyes on the ceiling, speaking as if I were not there. "I was too wild. Too adventurous. Too joyful." Now he looked at me. "I assumed it was a flaw in myself."

"Those qualities are not flaws. They are what I admire most about you."

His face softened but then agony flicked back across his features.

"They would disagree with you. When I came of age, they were only too happy to see me depart Pemberley. As there was never any danger of my inheriting Pemberley, I could travel or study. I extended my absence beyond what they thought acceptable. But at the moment of Thomas's accident, everything—" He crossed his arms hard across his chest.

I did not need to speak the words he could not say. The dilemma of his family had become real. The estate would go to a child born of scandal.

A log in the hearth popped.

"I am bound to duties not rightfully mine."

"You are a *Darcy*. Your *father's* son. He and Lady Anne ought to have treated you with kindness."

"Could *you* in such circumstances?" There was a pause during which I considered this, but he went on. "Of course *you* could. You are one of the most forgiving, kindest people that ever lived."

I laughed. "Me? I am constantly irate and judge everyone."

"Yet you *are* kind and you do forgive, though I do not know how."

"*Not* forgiving gnaws at me. And I find kindness a good distraction from my frustration at the world's unfairness."

"I could use distractions."

Our eyes locked, setting my heart racing.

"Thank you for trusting me with this secret."

"Not so secret if Miss Vane knows." He bit his bottom lip, an expression that made my legs weak.

"And now that she is cross with you, will she keep it?"

"I gave her land to buy her silence."

I sucked in a breath. "No!"

He flicked his hand as if swatting away a fly. "I have always loathed the house in Scotland, as has Georgiana. It is cold and forbidding, and filled with unpleasant memories and disagreeable neighbours. It shall not seem like a loss to my sister when I tell her." He winced. "She should know, she is old enough now."

His eyes searched mine as if looking for a promise that his beloved sister would not run from him and his shame.

I could keep my distance no longer. I rose, walking straight to him, and slid my hand into his. A simple gesture, but one I hoped would say all I could not, and one I hoped he would not reject.

For a moment, he stood frozen, then he squeezed my hand. I exhaled with relief.

"Why do you not run from me? Born of scandal. Unwanted."

"Not unwanted." I reached out with my free hand and touched his cheek.

He closed his eyes and leant into my palm, making me smile.

He opened his eyes again. "The most I have ever felt myself was with you. For years, I have pushed you away, thinking it was the right thing to do. That to continue the

Darcy legacy, I could not be who I am. Yet I am not what or who *you* thought I was."

"I never cared about your lands, and I certainly do not care about your past. I care about you. I care *for* you!"

He squeezed my hand again and almost smiled.

"Mr Darcy, this is an opportunity to embrace your truest self. I have said it, as has your cousin: there are none left to judge you. Not in the way you fear. The rest are unimportant."

"How can you say that? Members of society—"

"Do you respect them or desire their favour?"

"No."

"Then it matters not who your mother was. You are a *Darcy* and Pemberley is rightly yours. Your mother acknowledged you as her son. There is nothing scandalous about any of that. Allow yourself the happiness and freedom afforded you by the fortune you have inherited."

"There is only one happiness I desire." And with that, he leant in and kissed me.

It was like my insides were filled with little bubbles, rising and popping. I thought I might float away. Nothing in my life had ever felt as perfect as when he was kissing me. I sank into him, returning the kiss, relieved and hopeful that at last we could be together. He pressed his hands against my back, pulling me tighter as the kiss deepened. I lost myself in the feel of his lips, warm and soft, brushing against mine. My heart raced and I fought back a smile.

A moment later, his hands wandered lower. I froze and he stepped back. "My apologies. I have struggled to control myself when I am with you."

He looked regretful. Worried he would turn and leave, I wanted to reach out and pull him back to me but instead I took his hand and clasped it in both of mine.

"No, you may not run away from me. Not again." He sighed, looking at our entwined hands before meeting my eyes. "I need...I need to understand how you feel about us. What are your intentions, for I can no longer bear this game. You kiss me and then leave me, over and over. I love you, but I will let you go if—"

"You love me?" His eyes darkened and his grasp on my hands tightened.

I pressed my lips together. The words had tumbled out without my realising. To admit my feelings was to be vulnerable, but he had been so with me in sharing his painful confessions. And I did love him. "Yes," was all I said.

He blinked. He blinked faster, the corners of his lips twitching. I thought he might cry, but a man such as Mr Darcy—would he allow tears to fall? He swallowed hard. "After all I have told you, you still love me? I am not the man you thought I was."

"I loved you before I knew who you were. I have loved you ever since we met, but you kept me at a distance."

"I can do so no longer." He pulled me to him, enfolding me in his arms, kissing and kissing me, and this time, keeping his hands where they caused no alarm.

We caught our breath, foreheads pressed together. "I love you, Elizabeth Bennet. You are all I have dreamt of but would not allow myself." He took both my hands in his, lifted them, and kissed the tips of my fingers. "'Your two great eyes will slay me suddenly. Their beauty shakes me who was once serene'."

I sighed happily. "Which poet?"

"Chaucer. It is as if he read my heart." He kissed my knuckles and gazed at me fondly. Happiness rendered him ever more handsome. "Dearest, loveliest Elizabeth, would you do me the honour of becoming my wife?"

"Yes," I said without thinking. I gasped. So often I had yearned for this moment, despairing it would never happen, yet he had asked at last. Was I dreaming? No. The question was as real as the hands still holding mine. "I would be honoured to be your wife."

His eyes lit up with joy, but still he asked, "Are you certain? If the truth gets out—"

I took his cheeks in my hands. "It cannot alter my love for you."

He smiled almost shyly, and then more broadly before leaning in and kissing me once again. "I wish not to be parted from you ever again. We ought to marry soon. Let us get a licence and do it this week."

"This week? I do not believe we can marry so fast. There are invitations, and gowns and—"

His lips traced the length of my neck, down to my clavicle, nudging at the fabric of my bodice. "A month. No more."

"A month," I whispered, my body burning and heart overflowing. "I promise."

EPILOGUE

Four years later

The sun shone bright and warm after days of rain, so we were thrilled to be out of doors.

"The weather was far better in Italy," I said.

"And Greece," Darcy said, shading his eyes. "Mary, this way!"

Little Mary teetered then toddled after us on the expanse of grass leading to Pemberley's gardens.

"When might we return?"

"After the baby is born," Darcy said, cupping his hand against my protruding belly.

"You said that the last time."

"And you insisted on expecting again."

"Insisted?" I slapped his hand away, smiling. "It was a mutual venture."

He pulled me close, stooping to nuzzle his nose against my neck. "An *enjoyable* venture."

I nodded, holding him tight.

Our early married days had been like a spring thaw as Darcy let go of the anger and fear he had held onto for so long and grew to accept the security of the deep love and warm happiness he now shared with me. As with spring's temperamental weather, there were occasional storms that returned layers of frost and anxiety. At those times, he would retreat into himself and brood over questions of his mother's fate, and what he saw as unmet expectations and duties still to be fulfilled. He did not wish to share his thoughts, but I was persistent. I chased him into the woods, into his study, and on one occasion, into the pouring rain, demanding that he speak to me and insisting that he allow himself the joy he deserved. By some miracle that I shall never take for granted, each argument ended in kisses and thoughtful words and the emergence of his brilliant smile. Sometimes I wished I could go back in time and tell a younger Elizabeth—the one who watched him walk away on the hill looking over Meryton after being told of his brother's death—that all would be well, that he would love me, and that I would be allowed to love him back.

Leaving England after our wedding to travel abroad was our mutual idea; each of us had long desired to explore other lands. Prior to our engagement, when he had planned to go alone to the Continent, Darcy had presented his cousin with a plan for maintaining the estates in his absence. He knew the colonel was as proficient with tenants as he had been with his fellow soldiers, and Mrs Fitzwilliam was a brilliant partner in his endeavours, so we departed mostly at ease. Georgiana remained in London under the strict but kind guidance of her new companion, Mrs Annesley, and her aunt, Lady Matlock.

After we crossed the sea, Darcy became once again the man I had met at Longbourn: curious, carefree, loving, passionate. The time without family or society did us both good. He could indulge—and share with me—his ardent interest in history, ruins, and ancient poetry, and listen to my thoughts and ideas on, well, nearly anything. I was thrilled to learn that there was even more depth and kindness to him than I could have imagined, and with him, my own restlessness quieted.

His night terrors took me by surprise—they had apparently plagued him for years. I would awaken to find him thrashing and calling out to his brother, his mother, and his father. At first—stating he did not wish to burden me and that he had grown accustomed to these horrible dreams—he desired to sleep away from me, to lock himself in private and suffer alone. I refused to let him go, affirming my belief that the purpose of marriage was to share burdens. I would take his hands in mine and kiss his knuckles, stroke his face, whisper kindnesses, pour him some brandy—any and all I could to bring him back to the world. He corrected my assumption that the dreams were of missing his family, though I ought to have known. Instead, he dreamt that his deceased relations pinned him under water or clawed at him as he attempted to climb a cliff. The worst dream was of being sealed into a coffin by their hands. It broke my heart to watch him suffer so, but I held him and listened. Over time, he settled more quickly; eventually, the terrible dreams subsided. We still keep a bottle of spirits on my bedside table, though it is not needed nearly as often as in the beginning of our marriage.

We always sleep touching in some fashion: hands clasped, legs entwined, or curled into each other. I sometimes lie next to my beloved husband and ache with regret that my sister Mary will never know such love. She had wondered what it would be like to press her body against a man's. If only I could tell her that it surpassed our imagining.

I was already increasing when we returned to England. We were in Greece when I told Darcy of my suspicions and, thrilled and concerned, he immediately began preparations for the journey home. We arrived in London in time to celebrate Georgiana's wedding to Mr William Bexley. Though she was only eighteen years of age and we thought her rather young for marriage, the couple was extremely well-suited and we feared causing them unhappiness with a protracted engagement, knowing our years apart had not been for the better. Their wedding was simple by the standards of the *ton*, but lovely and heartfelt, and their happiness enhanced ours.

I gave birth at Grosvenor Street with Jane at my side. Six weeks later, the tanned skin we had earned on our travels now faded, Darcy and I and our new daughter journeyed north to Pemberley, the Darcy ancestral home my husband had long felt unworthy to claim as his own.

We had spent weeks and hours discussing his mixed feelings about the estate where he was raised and where the mother he never knew had worked. Our minds worked as one when making decisions about the rooms where we would sleep, those we would redecorate, and how we would ensure the Darcy name was passed onto our children in a house of love, laughter, esteem, and happiness.

With the joy we took in each other, both intellectually and physically, it seemed I would likely be expecting over and over. The idea of a large family pleased me, but not if creating one entirely replaced adventures abroad, nor if my husband worried so. I hoped he would come to view my condition less tenuously, for women with fewer resources did far more than those of our class and still bore their children successfully.

A sharp cry from little Mary interrupted my reverie. She had tripped over small roots around my favourite willow and was now bellowing. Darcy let go of my hand and scooped her up, brushing off her knees and bouncing her until she forgot her woes. "Come, darling," he said to her, "let us see how the peas are growing."

"Peas!" cried Mary.

Darcy had feared he would be a cold, uncaring parent, but in this, I had reassured him as well. "How can a man such as you, with warmth and love so plentiful, imagine that that love would not be passed on to a child?" I said it again and again, but he had to become a father to believe it. His fretful dreams returned as my confinement approached, but vanished soon after.

The moment he first held Mary Agatha Darcy, he melted. He had asked if her middle name might be that of the woman who had given birth to him. Before we left for the Continent, Darcy had hired an investigator to discover what he could of his birth mother. We learnt that Agatha had been her Christian name, and that she had not killed herself as he had been told, but had died only months after his birth. Once dismissed from Pemberley, she had found employment at a factory in Manchester, where the lack of heat and long hours of physical labour affected her severely and her health deteriorated.

I feared bestowing her name on our child might bring my husband unneeded pain, but he promised it would not, and felt the need to pay tribute to her. As my father had a great-aunt Agatha, our families and friends assumed our daughter had been named after that relation, and we never corrected them.

Only Georgiana and the Fitzwilliams knew the complete truth. Darcy told his sister all upon our return from our travels. He did not believe she would betray his trust nor turn her back on him, and she did not. They were both keepers of Darcy family secrets, and I believe this created a stronger bond of mutual affection between them.

Darcy carried the now-soothed Mary towards the garden. Each day the weather permitted, we checked the progress of vegetables in a corner that had been planted just for her enjoyment. The gardeners had suggested plants that a toddler might tug at and crush, and whose progress she might notice most readily. Her favourites were the peas, for the tendrils crept up the tent of strings set for that purpose, and each visit brought new wonders. The softness in Darcy's face as he witnessed our first-born's discovery of the world melted my heart daily.

Mary had been wanting to come out for days and did not understand why getting wet was frowned upon. Perhaps we ought to have allowed it, for in my youth, I had splashed in puddles and marched through storms. Yet she was still very young. When she was a bit older, I hoped she might do as she pleased. I would attempt to convince Darcy that she needed the freedom of body and spirit that was within the bounds of propriety, though watching him set her down to explore made me think he might not need to much convincing.

Darcy and Mary continued on to her beloved vegetable plants, but I wandered away towards the formal garden. The manicured hedges cut like exotic animals reminded me of museum visits with Mrs Lambert. While I did not miss pining for Mr Darcy and despairing at my loneliness, I did look back on my time with the former Miss Festing in London and the outings her mother had treated us to with great fondness, and determined to take Mary and our subsequent children on enriching cultural adventures.

I wandered on, loving the patch of wildflowers. Jane's two small boys had picked some for her at Bingley's behest when they had come to visit some months earlier; she had beamed as if they had brought her the finest jewels.

I heard Mary shrieking and returned to the cutting garden. She was holding a pod aloft. "Peas!"

Darcy nibbled at the pod she held between her stubby fingers, which sent her to shrieking with joy once again. His smile was all softness and joy, and that could not have made me happier.

"Mrs Darcy." A servant approached with a letter.

I sat upon the nearest garden bench to read it and soon looked up and called to my husband. "Another young woman in need."

"Are there any rooms open at Rosebay?"

I nodded absently, perusing the details of the woman's plea, and considering the possibilities. We had secured a large house in Middlesex as a home for unwed mothers to give birth and return to service. Miss Mitchell, Georgiana's former maid, now worked there teaching young women how to care for the babes they chose to keep—a choice she had made—and assisted in the discreet placement of infants with families we hoped would be loving.

We also had purchased the very factory where Agatha had worked after leaving Darcy at Pemberley. Under my husband's guidance, it was made as safe as could be by shortening hours without lessening pay, fixing broken windows, and adding more sources of heat and air. In addition, he was overseeing the renovations of two outbuildings to provide decent, if modest, housing for the workers. We had turned the house on its grounds into a home for women in need while they were in their confinements, after which, those who so desired were sent to the factory to learn to run the machines. Many gave their children away, but some were earning enough to keep them.

Darcy and I spoke of creating a children's home akin to the London Foundling Hospital, which I had so admired, but that would have to wait. Even a modest facility would require time to build, and as my husband would remind me, especially when I showed signs of fatigue, we were busy building a young family.

I re-read the letter. "Poor thing." I looked up at him. "Rosebay has room for nineteen women, and seventeen are being cared for currently."

"Seventeen? That seems impossible."

"You say that every time I offer a number."

"I simply did not expect so many women to be in need of our help. How is it possible?"

"Remember us in our early married days?"

"*Early* days?" He gave me a rakish grin. "I would take you now if not for Mary's presence."

We laughed, knowing it was true. More than one servant had come upon us in the gardens, the carriage, and the occasional alcove while we were in a most compromising position.

"Young lovers and their passions will not be quelled, Darcy."

I thought of when we first met, and how easy it might have been to turn those stolen kisses in the woods into something more, and how a lapse in judgment could so easily lead to ruination. I took his hand as we watched Mary pick at the dirt. "I wish there was more I could do."

"You do more than most."

"But is it enough?"

He wrapped his arms around me, and I wished all could enjoy moments of calm and enjoyment such as this. "For now, yes. You are good to our servants; you are raising one nearly perfect child with another on the way. And another after that, I hope. And you love me, far more than I deserve."

I kissed his cheek. "That last bit is a lie."

A magpie streaked overhead chattering its loud 'ch-tak' that sounded like laughter. Some said they were a symbol of good luck and fortune. I thought they were simply a noisy nuisance. I had all the good luck and fortune I could ever ask for. Even so, I would never chase the magpies away.

"Darcy?"

"Yes, my dear wife?"

"Shall we bring Mary to her nurse and spend some time alone before supper?"

He kissed my hand. "When have I ever refused you?"

"Well—"

"Heavens, woman, let me compliment and love you without argument for once."

I shrugged. "Someday, perhaps."

We both laughed.

The End

ACKNOWLEDGMENTS

Thanks to Amy D'Orazio and Jan Ashton for endless editorial and historical assistance. Your knowledge is incredible, and your advice invaluable. To Jennifer Altman and the Quills & Quartos community for authorly support and inspiration. To my friends who always ask about my writing, and make a girl feel special when a new book comes out. To my students who make me laugh in a good way, and who act like my being an author is interesting. To Sage and Joanna for being the coolest kids I could have asked for. To Jonathan for planning a *Pride & Prejudice* tour of Derbyshire for me, and not laughing when I took a billion pics of it all.

ABOUT THE AUTHOR

Michelle Ray is a middle school English teacher who also directs plays, writes stories, and sees as many Broadway shows as she can. She grew up in Los Angeles and went to the awesome Westlake School for Girls where theater had the cachet of football and the girls were in charge of everything. She lives with her husband near Washington DC, has two wonderful grown daughters, and dreams of traveling anywhere and everywhere. She is the author of several novels, including Quills & Quartos' *There You Were*.

For more about her writing, go to www.michelleraybooks.com

- facebook.com/michelle.ray.1042
- amazon.com/stores/Michelle-Ray/author/B004AO30AE
- bookbub.com/authors/michelle-ray

ALSO BY MICHELLE RAY

There You Were: A Pride & Prejudice Variation

Falling for Hamlet

A World on Fire

Outlaw

Much Ado About Something

Mac/Beth: The Price of Fame Shouldn't Be Murder